SCHOOL CRIME AND SAFETY

SCHOOL CRIME AND SAFETY

PETER W. AMHERST
EDITOR

Novinka Books
An imprint of Nova Science Publishers, Inc.
New York

For permission to use material from this book please contact us:
Telephone 631-231-7269; Fax 631-231-8175
Web Site: http://www.novapublishers.com

NOTICE TO THE READER

Library of Congress Cataloging-in-Publication Data:
Available Upon Request

ISBN: 1-59454-736-X

Published by Nova Science Publishers, Inc. ✢New York

CONTENTS

PREFACE

Schools are entrusted with ensuring the safety of students and staff. One measure of the safety of America's public schools is the presence of violence on school campuses. Violent incidents include rape, sexual battery other than rape, physical attacks or fights with and without a weapon, threats of physical attack with and without a weapon, and robberies with and without a weapon. In order to provide a measure of the most severe incidents, those crimes that would be considered aggravated assaults were included as serious violent incidents. This book examines school bullying, prevention of youth hate crimes and other safety plans and policies within schools.

In: School Crime and Safety ISBN 1-59454-736-X
Editor: Peter W. Amherst, pp. 1-22

Chapter 1

PREVENTING YOUTH HATE CRIME: A MANUAL FOR SCHOOLS AND COMMUNITIES*

U.S. Department of Education

INTRODUCTION

The term "hate crime" is defined by various federal and state laws. In its broadest sense, the term refers to an attack on an individual or his or her property (e.g., vandalism, arson, assault, murder) in which the victim is intentionally selected because of his or her race, color, religion, national origin, gender, disability, or sexual orientation.

Every year, thousands of Americans are victims of such hate crimes. Each one of these crimes has a ripple effect in our communities. The pain and injustice of such crimes tear at the fabric of our democratic society, creating fear and tensions that ultimately affect us all.

Schools are not immune from such intolerance and violence. Teenagers and young adults account for a significant proportion of the country's hate crimes-both as perpetrators and as victims. Hate-motivated behavior, whether in the form of ethnic conflict, harassment, intimidation, or graffiti, is often apparent on school grounds. Hate violence is also perpetrated by hate groups, which actively work to recruit young people to their ranks.

The good news is that children are not born with such attitudes; they are learned. It is possible for schools, families, law enforcement, and communities to work together to prevent the development of the prejudiced attitudes and violent behavior that lead to hate crimes. Prejudice and the resulting violence can be reduced or even eliminated by instilling in children an appreciation and respect for each other's differences, and by helping them to develop empathy, conflict resolution, and critical thinking skills. By teaching children that even subtle forms of hate are inherently wrong, we can hope to prevent more extreme acts of hate in the future.

Educators have a tremendous opportunity to reduce or eliminate hate-motivated crime and violence. A number of school districts and individual schools have already taken action to create comprehensive anti-hate policies and programs that involve every facet of the school community, students, parents, teachers, staff, and administrators. These schools have worked to create a school climate where hateful acts are not tolerated, and to provide an equitable, supportive, and safe environment for all students.

Preventing Youth Hate Crime: A Manual for Schools and Communities is intended to assist more schools and communities to confront and eliminate harassing, intimidating, violent, and other hate-motivated behavior among young people. It is intended to promote discussion, planning, immediate action, and long-term responses to hate crime. By understanding what hate-motivated behavior is and how best to respond to it, schools can become a powerful force in bringing such incidents to an end.

How Big a Problem is Hate Crime?

The FBI reports that approximately 10,700 hate crimes were reported in the United States in 1996-approximately 29 such incidents per day. (Since many hate crimes are never reported to police, it is likely that the actual number of hate crimes significantly exceeds this number.) About 70 percent of all reported hate crimes were crimes against a person; about 30 percent were property crimes. Research indicates that a substantial number of these crimes were committed by males under age 20.

---

* Excerpted from http://www.usdoj.gov/topical.htm, US Dept. of Education, Office of Elementary and Secondary Education Safe and Drug-Free Schools Program.

America's Students are Increasingly Diverse

School enrollment in 1997 has risen to a record 52.2 million students. Over the course of the next ten years, public high school enrollment is expected to increase by 13 percent. Many of these students will be enrolled in schools with increasing numbers of students from different races, ethnic backgrounds, and cultures. By the year 2007, Hispanic students will outnumber African American students by 2.5 percent. The numbers of Asian and Native American students are also expected to increase dramatically. The percentage of Caucasian students is expected to decline from 66 percent in 1997 to 61 percent in 2007. Within 25 years, 50 percent of all students will belong to a minority group.

ELEMENTS OF EFFECTIVE SCHOOL-BASED HATE PREVENTION PROGRAMS

A comprehensive hate prevention program will involve all school personnel in creating a school climate in which prejudice and hate-motivated behavior are not acceptable, but which also permits the expression of diverse viewpoints. Hate prevention, as used in this manual, means prevention of hate-motivated behavior and crimes.

1. Provide hate prevention training to all staff, including teachers, administrators, school security personnel, and support staff. All school employees, including teachers, administrators, support staff, bus drivers, and security staff, should be aware of the various manifestations of hate and be competent to address hate incidents. Training should include anti-bias and conflict resolution methods; procedures for identifying and reporting incidents of racial, religious, and sexual harassment, discrimination, and hate crime; strategies for preventing such incidents from occurring; and resources available to assist in dealing with these incidents.

2. Ensure that all students receive hate prevention training through age-appropriate classroom activities, assemblies, and other school-related activities. Prejudice and discrimination are learned attitudes and behaviors. Neither is uncontrollable or inevitable. Teaching children that even subtle forms of hate-such as ethnic slurs or epithets, negative or offensive name-calling, stereotyping, and exclusion-are hurtful and inherently wrong can help to prevent more extreme, violent manifestations of hate. Through structured classroom activities and programs, children can begin to develop

empathy, while practicing the critical thinking and conflict resolution skills needed to recognize and respond to various manifestations of hate behavior.

3. Develop partnerships with families, community organizations, and law enforcement agencies. Hate crime prevention cannot be accomplished by schools alone. School districts are encouraged to develop partnerships with parent groups, youth serving organizations, criminal justice agencies, victim assistance organizations, businesses, advocacy groups, and religious organizations. These partnerships can help identify resources available to school personnel to address hate incidents, raise community awareness of the issue, ensure appropriate responses to hate incidents, and ensure that youth receive a consistent message that hate-motivated behavior will not be tolerated.

4. Develop a hate prevention policy to distribute to every student, every student's family, and every employee of the school district. An effective hate prevention policy will promote a school climate in which racial, religious, ethnic, gender and other differences, as well as freedom of thought and expression, are respected and appreciated. The policy should be developed with the input of parents, students, teachers, community members, and school administrators. It should include a description of the types of behavior prohibited under the policy; the roles and responsibilities of students and staff in preventing and reporting hate incidents or crimes; the range of possible consequences for engaging in this type of behavior; and locations of resources in the school and community where students can go for help. It should respect diverse viewpoints, freedom of thought, and freedom of expression. Every student should be informed of the contents of the school district's policy on hate crime on an annual basis. School districts are advised to consult with an attorney in the course of developing such a policy.

5. Develop a range of corrective actions for those who violate school hate-prevention policies. School districts are encouraged to take a firm position against all injurious manifestations of hate, from ethnic slurs, racial epithets, and taunts, to graffiti, vandalism, discrimination, harassment, intimidation, and violence. School districts can develop a wide range of non-disciplinary corrective actions to respond to incidents, including counseling, parent conferences, community service, awareness training, or completion of a research paper on an issue related to hate, as well as disciplinary actions such as in-school suspension or expulsion. School officials should be prepared to contact local, state or federal civil rights officials to respond to more serious incidents and, in cases involving criminal activity or threat of criminal activity, should call the police.

6. Collect and use data to focus district-wide hate prevention efforts. Collection of data on the occurrence of school-based hate incidents or crimes will assist administrators and teachers to identify patterns and to more effectively implement hate prevention policies and programs. To obtain such data, school districts may include questions regarding hate crime on surveys they conduct related to school crime and discipline, as well as collect and analyze incident-based data on specific hate incidents and crimes. In the latter case, school districts are encouraged to work closely with local law enforcement personnel to collect uniform and consistent data on hate crime.

7. Provide structured opportunities for integration. Young people can begin to interact across racial and ethnic lines through school- supported organizations and activities. Multi-ethnic teams of students can work together on community service projects, to organize extracurricular events, or to complete class projects. High school students can participate in service-learning projects in which they tutor, coach, or otherwise assist younger students from diverse backgrounds.

Which Hate Crime and Civil Rights Laws Apply?

A number of federal and state laws prohibit acts or threats of violence, as well as harassment and discrimination, based on race, color, religion, national origin, sexual orientation, gender and/or disability. It is important to check with an attorney to ascertain the extent to which federal and state hate crime and civil rights laws may also apply in the school context. The applicable federal laws include the following:

18 U.S.C. Section 245. Section 245, the principal federal hate crime statute, prohibits intentional use of force or threat of force against a person because of his or her race, color, religion, or national origin, and because he or she was engaged in a "federally protected activity," such as enrolling in or attending any public school or college. Legislation has been introduced which would amend Section 245 to include crimes committed because of the victim's sexual orientation, gender or disability, and to eliminate the "federally protected activity" requirement.

Title VI of the Civil Rights Act of 1964. Title VI and regulations promulgated under Title VI prohibit discrimination by institutions that receive federal funding, including harassment, on the basis of race, color, and national origin.

Title IX of the Education Amendments of 1972. Title IX and regulations promulgated under Title IX prohibit discrimination by institutions that receive federal funding, including harassment, based on sex.

Section 504 of the Rehabilitation Act of 1973. Section 504 and regulations promulgated under Section 504 prohibit discrimination by institutions that receive federal funding, including harassment, based on disability.

EXAMPLES OF HATE PREVENTION PROGRAMS

The following hate prevention programs are examples of the measures that educators can take to address hatemotivated behavior in their schools and communities. These examples are not exhaustive, but are intended to assist educators in determining which programs might work best in their own schools and communities. For additional information, please contact the individuals listed.

The programs, activities, organizations, curricula, books, web sites, videos and other resources listed in this Manual are not exhaustive, nor is their inclusion intended as an endorsement by the Department of Justice or the Department of Education. Rather, these listings are intended to assist educators in determining which programs, activities, organizations, or instructional materials might be most suitable for their own classrooms, schools, and communities.

New Jersey Department of Education: Project PRIDE

In 1995, 885 bias incidents against African Americans, Hispanics, and Jews were reported in New Jersey. In response, the State Department of Education's (NJDOE) Office of Bilingual and Equity Issues, in conjunction with the Holocaust Education Commission, the NAACP, the National Conference, the Anti-Defamation League, and county Human Relations Commissions, developed Project PRIDE (Peace, Respect, Inclusion, Diversity and Equity).

PRIDE's goal is to eliminate bias incidents from public schools. PRIDE trains parents, students, and teachers to understand the dynamics of institutional racism, discrimination, bias crime, and hate-motivated conflict. Key aspects of the Project include conflict resolution training for teachers and other school staff anti-bias and conflict resolution training for students; and school-wide support for principles of non-violence.

PRIDE is currently being used in 122 New Jersey school districts. NJDOE hopes to implement PRIDE statewide in coming years.

Contact:
Iliana Okum, Project Director. 609/292-8777.
Los Angeles, California: Educating for Diversity

In 1992, the Los Angeles Unified School District (LAUSD) approved a plan to address diversity and cultural issues in its schools. The Board of Education's action plan, Educating for Diversity: A Framework for Multicultural and Human Relations Education, was implemented in 1994 and includes guidelines, strategies, and resources for addressing these issues in the district's instructional program.

The LAUSD plan consists of a multi-prong approach that addresses the needs of teachers, administrators, students, and the community. Teams of teachers from each school site receive training on district data collection procedures. School counselors receive additional training on working with victims of hate crimes, and parents are offered a one-day orientation on family and human relations issues.

Two classroom curricula have been implemented to improve students' understanding of and respect for diversity. Sixth and ninth graders receive a 10-20 week curriculum entitled Healthy Relations, which emphasizes multicultural and human relations sensitivity, gender relations, conflict resolution, peer mediation, and media literacy. Different and the Same, a video series on diversity and inclusion, has been provided as a teaching tool in the elementary school grades.

Contact:
Evangelina Stockwell, Assistant Superintendent, Office of Intergroup Relations. 213/625-6579.

Oakland, Richmond, and Berkeley, California: Youth Together Project

The Youth Together Project was developed by a coalition of human rights groups, teachers, school administrators, parents, and students, in response to reports of increasing racial and ethnic tensions among youth in the Oakland, Richmond, and Berkeley schools.

The Project aims to foster cross-cultural understanding between different ethnic groups; establish preventive programs designed by and for youth; and influence hate crime policy within participating school districts. Students are grouped into multicultural teams to examine individual stereotypes and prejudices through group discussions and cooperative learning activities. This approach is based upon the theories that the keys to resolving ethnic tensions among students is to understand student perspectives on race, power, and privilege, and to address the institutional roots of racial violence in the schools. Teams work together to implement hate and violence prevention programs, such as a peer education program.

During its first year, the Project recruited and trained 75 students from five high schools (15 students from each school) to serve on the multicultural teams. Over a one-year period, the teams developed, conducted, and analyzed a survey of 2,500 Bay Area students' views on violence and racial tension in their schools. The team members then published educational materials on issues of race, equity, and school violence. These materials are available upon request.

Contact:
Margaretta Lin, Project Director. 510/834-9455. www.arc99.com

Omaha, Staten Island, San Diego, and Los Angeles: Stop the Hate

A WORLD OF DIFFERENCE Institute's Stop the Hate program, developed by the Anti-Defamation League, is being pilot tested in one high school and several feeder schools in Omaha, Staten Island, San Diego, and Los Angeles.

Stop the Hate is designed to combat hate-related incidents by altering how schools respond to inter-group tensions. The program is based on the premise that the first step that schools must take to stop hate violence is to acknowledge the reality of hate crimes. Schools then develop a voluntary "code of conduct" that clearly communicates that acts of hate will not be tolerated by the school community.

Stop the Hate provides comprehensive, anti-bias, and conflict resolution training for high school students, teachers, administrators, parents, and community members. A key component of the program is prevention training for all stakeholders-including development of the necessary skills to identify, understand, and effectively prevent hate crimes. Youth are directly involved in the program as trainers and peer leaders.

Contact:
Lucia Rodriguez, Project Director. 212/885-7818. *www.adl.org/AWOD/AWOD.html*

Los Angeles, Revere, Memphis, New York: Facing History and Ourselves (FHAO)

For more than 20 years, FHAO has been working with middle and secondary school educators to assist them in examining issues of hate, intolerance, compassion, courage, and individual responsibility in the classroom. FHAO annually reaches more than 900,000 students in urban, suburban, and rural communities across the United States.

In California, students in 50 of the middle and secondary schools within the Los Angeles Unified School District examine prejudice, discrimination, and related issues through an FHAO course integrated into the American and world history, literature, and arts curricula, as well as through service learning.

In Revere, Massachusetts, an urban area outside Boston, teachers worked with FHAO to develop an interdisciplinary English and social studies program aimed at increasing student awareness about diversity and reducing prejudice. Every ninth grade student participates in this program.

In Memphis, Tennessee, high school students at White Station High School coordinated discussion sessions with teachers, community leaders, and parents about confronting social isolation and building community. FHAO has provided in-service training for teachers to infuse citizenship training into the high school's curriculum and improve cultural understanding.

At the International High Schools within New York's Public School System, all new students receive an in depth FHAO course as a foundation for learning about citizenship and building interpersonal skills. This course is integrated into the literature and history curriculum.

Contact:
Margot Strom, Executive Director. 617/232-1595. *www.facing.org.*

Tucson, Arizona: El Hogar De La Paz (The Home of Peace)

In 1996, the Tucson Unified School District, in collaboration with five other school districts, developed a comprehensive program to address escalating ethnic and racial conflict in Tuscon and Pima Counties. Funded by a grant from the U.S. Department of Education's Safe and Drug Free Schools Program, the program provides a range of services to all schools throughout the county, as well as specialized programs tailored to the unique needs of particular schools and classrooms. The program provides:

- One- and two-day coalition-building seminars for teachers and students, designed to help them lead and facilitate group discussions on racial and ethnic issues, and address intergroup conflict;
- A cadre of certified trainers within each district who are available to conduct anti-bias, peer mediation, and conflict resolution training for teachers and students in their district's schools;
- One- and two-day workshops for students on diversity issues and cross-cultural relations;
- Quarterly newsletters, distributed to all teachers in the county, with information on diversity and conflict resolution activities for the classroom, responding to bias incidents, and related issues;
- An anti-hate web site, developed by students (*http://instech.tusd.kiz.az.us/peace/index.htm*); and
- Training and written materials for law enforcement, local government agencies, and community organizations to increase awareness about identifying, reporting, and responding to hate crime, and assisting victims.

In the two years since its inception, more than 750 students, 700 school staff, 200 law enforcement personnel, and 150 local government and community staff have participated in workshops organized by El Hogar de la Paz.

Contact:
Dennis W. Noonan, Project Coordinator. 520/512-3084.

Orange County, California: Bridges of Understanding

The Orange County Human Relations Council is a nonprofit organization which counts among its members corporations, cities, foundations, the county, schools, and the courts. For over ten years, the Council has worked with schools at all levels to help build inter-ethnic communication, cohesion, a sense of community, and a safe, inclusive climate throughout the County's schools.

To accomplish these goals in a sustainable manner, the Council works collaboratively with each school on an individual basis for a minimum of three years. A leadership team works with the school community to assess that school's needs and to create a school human relations task force. In conjunction with the task force, the Council then provides training sessions for parents, students, administrators, school staff, and teachers. The Council also works with the task force to design student retreats and schoolwide projects.

These programs are supported by a county-wide summer youth leadership institute; annual middle and high school student symposia on inter-cultural cooperation; a school inter-ethnic relations round table; and a parent leadership institute designed to build the skills of non-English speaking parents so that they can be more effectively involved in their children's schools.

The Council currently provides comprehensive school inter-ethnic relations and violence prevention programs in 41 Orange County schools, and reaches over 21,000 students and teachers each year. Building Bridges of Understanding, the Council's school inter-ethnic relations program, is funded by corporate and private contributions totaling $500,000 annually.

Contact:
Rusty Kennedy, Executive Director. 714/567-7470.

Classroom Activities and Discussion Topics

The following activities illustrate the sort of classroom projects that can help students develop empathy, critical thinking skills, and an awareness and appreciation for diversity. A number of anti-bias curricula have been developed by various organizations which contain additional activities; these curricula are listed in the Bibliography at the end of this Manual.

In order to be most effective, such classroom activities should be part of a comprehensive hate prevention strategy that involves all members of the school communityincluding the student body, parents, school administration, law enforcement, and community organizations. Issues such as prejudice, discrimination, and hate crime cannot be effectively addressed in the classroom alone. Rather, classroom lessons must be reinforced by the school community, and beyond.

It can sometimes be difficult for teachers and students to discuss issues such as prejudice and discrimination, particularly in a multicultural setting. Therefore, prior to engaging in these or other anti-bias teaching activities, teachers may wish to receive diversity or conflict resolution training.

Elementary School Activities

Reading books aloud is an excellent way to prompt classroom discussions about the diversity of cultures, traditions, and lifestyles in our society. Books also help children to develop empathy by helping them to understand the points of view of other people.

An annotated bibliography of multicultural children's literature is available from A WORLD OF DIFFERENCE Institute, Anti-Defamation League, 823 United Nations Plaza, New York, NY, 10017. 212/885-7800; or 800/343-5540.

Encouraging children's critical thinking ability may be one of the best antidotes to prejudice. Help children recognize instances of prejudice, discrimination, and stereotyping, and discuss appropriate responses to such attitudes and behaviors when they encounter them. Newspapers, magazines, movies, and television news and entertainment shows can provide opportunities for classroom discussion.

A web site that introduces children to concepts of prejudice and discrimination in an interactive, age-appropriate format, Hateful Acts Hurt Kids, can be found at www.usdoj.gov/kidspage. This web site helps children learn empathy, an appreciation for diversity, and coping skills should they become victims of prejudice.

A free pamphlet on talking to young children about prejudice and discrimination is available from the National PTA, 300 North Wabash Avenue, Suite 2100, Chicago, IL, 60611. 312/670-6782.

Young children can work together to create positive change through community-oriented projects. Class projects such as painting over graffiti, or working together to develop a classroom code of conduct (e.g., "No child shall be teased or excluded because of his or her race, religion, accent, ethnicity, disability, gender, or appearance."), all affirm children's ability to take a stand against prejudiced thinking.

Additional hate prevention activities for elementary grades can be found in "Teacher They Called Me A _______!", available for $12.50 from the Anti-Defamation League, 22D Hollywood Avenue, Hohokus, NJ, 07423. 800/343-5540, or 212/885-7951; Starting Small: Teaching Tolerance in Preschool and the Early Grades, available free of charge from Teaching Tolerance, 400 Washington Avenue, Montgomery, AL, 36104. 334/264-0286; and Actions Speak Louder Than Words, available free of charge from the National Conference, 71 Fifth Avenue, New York, NY, 10003. 800/352-6225.

Middle and Secondary School Activities

By learning what youth and communities can do to reduce or prevent hate violence, students learn that their choices and actions can have an impact. People working together to stop hate violence across the nation have made a big difference. The movement against hate groups and hate violence includes hundreds of national, regional, and local organizations. In particular, young people can bring to a community an increased awareness of the problems of prejudice.

To convey the power of community mobilization against hate crime, you might show the award-winning video Not In Our Town, which documents community resistance to anti-Semitic and other hate crimes in Billings, Montana. You may wish to ask questions such as: Who are the victims, bystanders, and perpetrators in this film? What form of resistance did the community initiate? How did the organized hate group members react to the union of Jews and non-Jews in the community? Do you think it is true that the community "found a weapon more powerful than [the KKK's]?" What was that weapon, and what made it more powerful? Has this, or another, type of bigotry ever occurred in your community? What, if any, forms of community action were used to combat it?

Not In Our Town is available with a teaching guide from The Working Group, 510/268-9675, ext. 317. More on community mobilization projects can be found in Teaching Tolerance Magazine, a free semiannual magazine providing educators with resources for promoting interracial and intercultural understanding. Teachers and other educators can subscribe free of charge using official school letterhead. Teaching Tolerance, 400

Washington Avenue, Montgomery, AL, 36104. 334/264-0286. Fax: 334/264-7310.

By understanding the various manifestations of hate throughout our nation's history, students learn to recognize it in contemporary society. Members of racial or religious groups, immigrants, women, the disabled, and gays and lesbians have been the targets of bigotry at various times in our country's history. Regardless of the specific identity or characteristics of the victims or perpetrators, however, there are elements common to all forms of intolerance and persecution.

You might have students research historical incidents of bigotry against particular groups, and present their reports to the class. Students can discuss what these reports show about why some people do not accept individuals who are different than themselves, and what individuals, groups, and our Nation have done to respond to acts of intolerance (e.g., civil rights laws, hate crime laws, the United Nations Manifesto on Human Rights).

Additional activities on the historical role of hate are suggested in Free At Last: A History of the Civil Rights Movement and Those Who Died in the Struggle, available free of charge from Teaching Tolerance, 400 Washington Avenue, Montgomery, AL, 36104. 334/264-0286; and in Facing History and Ourselves, from Facing History and Ourselves National Foundation, Inc., 16 Hurd Road, Brookline, MA, 02146. 617/232-1595.

Students can learn critical thinking skills to identify stereotyping that they encounter in their own lives, as well as in the media, literature, music, movies, and elsewhere.

More hate prevention activities for middle school students can be found in the award-winning Healing the Hate: A National Bias Crime Prevention Curriculum for Middle Schools, available for $26.00 from the Department of Justice's Office of Juvenile Justice and Delinquency Prevention, 800/638-8736; and in The Prejudice Book, available for $18.00 from the AntiDefamation League, Hohokus, NJ. 800/343-5540.

Resource Organizations

Anti-Defamation League (ADL). The ADL is a human relations organization with 31 regional offices across the country. ADL is dedicated to promoting intergroup cooperation and interfaith understanding. ADL's WORLD OF DIFFERENCE Institute has developed several K-12 curricula, fact sheets, and research materials, and has worked with numerous schools across the country to design comprehensive, school-wide policies to foster cultural awareness and increased appreciation for diversity. Over 300,000 children have participated in ADL and WORLD OF DIFFERENCE programs. Materials may be purchased from ADL's Anti-Bias/Diversity Catalog for Classroom and Community. 823 United Nations Plaza, New York, NY, 100 17. 212/490-2525; or, to order materials, 800/343-5540.

Center for Democratic Renewal (CDR). CDR is a national clearinghouse of information on the white supremacist movement, and provides training to schools, churches, community organizations, and law enforcement agencies. Over 40 publications are available, including the resource manual, When Hate Groups Come To Town, and the bimonthly newsletter, The Monitor. P.O. Box 50469, Atlanta, GA, 30302. 404/221-0025.

U.S. Department of Education. The Office for Civil Rights (OCR) provides legal guidance, technical assistance, and materials on racial and sexual harassment in school settings. The Office of Elementary and Secondary Education's Safe and Drug-Free Schools Program (SDFSP) provides discretionary and formula grant funding to state and local education agencies, governors' offices, and public and private nonprofit organizations for a wide range of school- and community-based drug and violence prevention efforts. 600 Independence Avenue, SW, Washington, D.C., 20202. OCR800/421-3481; SDFSP-202/260-3954.

U.S. Department of Justice. The Community Relations Service (CRS), a unique component of the Department of Justice, was established by the Civil Rights Act of 1964 to prevent or resolve community conflicts arising from actions or policies perceived to be discriminatory on the basis of race, color, or national origin. CRS provides a variety of services to schools and other community organizations, including conflict resolution, conciliation, and mediation training for students, teachers, and school administrators. 600 E Street NW, Suite 2000, Washington, D.C., 20530. 202/305-2935.

Educators For Social Responsibility (ESR). ESR creates and disseminates publications and programs for teachers and students emphasizing dialogue, critical thinking skills, nonviolent conflict resolution, social responsibility, and cooperation. ESR provides resources addressing intergroup relations, violence prevention, and character education. Teachers guides, textbooks, and videos are available. 23 Garden Street, Cambridge, MA, 02138. 800/370-2515.

Facing History and Ourselves (FHAO). For over twenty years, FHAO has used the lessons of history to teach young people the skills and attitudes necessary to be responsible and involved citizens and to preserve freedom. From its regional offices in Chicago, Memphis, Boston, New York, and Los Angeles, FHAO has developed programs for numerous schools across the country. FHAO provides schools with programs, resources, and speakers that relate history to contemporary issues. In addition, FHAO provides one- and two-day workshops, as well as week-long institutes, for educators; assists teachers to design their own course or plan lessons to enhance courses they are already teaching; and publishes a variety of curricula and other materials. 16 Hurd Road, Brookline, MA, 02146. 617/232-1595.

Green Circle Program. Green Circle develops programs to promote awareness, understanding, and appreciation of diversity in schools and other settings across the country. These programs encourage young people ages 12 to 18 to explore the dynamics of difference and discrimination, language, stereotypes, and the impact of historical and current events. 1300 Spruce Street, Philadelphia, PA. 215/893-8400.

National Association for the Advancement of Colored People (NAACP). The NAACP has over 2,200 chapters nationwide. Its principal objective is to ensure the educational, political, social, and economic equality of minority group citizens of the United States. The NAACP is committed to achieving these goals through non-violence. 4805 Mount Hope Drive, Baltimore, MD, 21215. 410/359-8900.

National Conference (NC). Formerly known as the National Conference of Christians and Jews, the NC was founded in 1927 to combat racism and religious bigotry, and to improve communications between different American communities. Its publication, Actions Speak Louder Than Words: A Skills-Based Curriculum for Building Inclusivity, available free of charge, is designed for use in elementary and middle schools. 71 Fifth Avenue, New York, NY, 10003. 212/807-8440, or 800/352-6225.

National Education Association (NEA). The NEA:s Human and Civil Rights Division (HCR) has primary responsibility for the Association's Safe Schools Program. An important component of the program is preventing and responding to hate-motivated incidents in schools. In addressing school safety in general, and hate-motivated behavior in particular, HCR provides training, technical assistance, and information to Association members and the public. 1201 16th Street, NW, Washington, D.C., 20036-3290. 202/822-7453.

National Hate Crime Prevention Project. The Project is funded jointly by the U.S. Department of Justice's Office of Juvenile Justice and Delinquency Prevention and the U.S. Department of Education's Safe and Drug Free Schools Program. The Project has developed Preventing Hate Crime: A Multidisciplinary Approach, which brings together educators, law enforcement and victim assistance professionals, policymakers, members of the religious community, and youth to develop strategies to prevent hate crime in their communities. The Project has also worked with the Congress of National Black Churches to respond to the arsons of African American churches, formed a Hate Crime Prevention Information Sharing Network, and developed Healing the Hate: A National Bias Crime Curriculum for Middle Schools. Educational Development Center, 55 Chapel Street, Newton, MA, 02158-1060. 800/225-4276; 617/969-7 100, x. 2534.

National Youth Advocacy Coalition (NYAC). NYAC, established in 1993, seeks to end discrimination against young people who are gay, lesbian, bisexual, or transgender. Among other activities, NYAC works with schools to address anti-gay behavior on campus, and provides hotline, resource, and referral information to students. 1711 Connecticut Avenue, NW, Suite 206, Washington, D.C., 20009. 202/319-7596, Parents, Families and Friends of Lesbians and Gays (PFLAG). PFLAG recognizes that sexual minority youth often feel unsafe in their school or community because they are targets of anti-gay attitudes. PFLAG aims to give these young people safe places to learn and grow, and mentoring relationships with caring adults. PFLAG is organized in over 400 communities in every state. Local volunteers offer peer support for gay. lesbian, bisexual, and transgender youth, their parents, family members and friends, and work with school and community leaders to address the needs of families with gay or lesbian members. 1011 14th Street, NW, Suite 1030, Washington, D.C., 20005. 202/638-4200.

Study Circles Resource Center (SCRC). SCRC helps communities use study circles-small, democratic, highly participatory discussions-to discuss and engage in problem solving on issues such as race, crime, education, youth issues, and American diversity. SCRC is currently working with over 50 communities nationwide to plan and implement study circle programs on race relations. Several SCRC materials are available free of charge for use in middle and upper grades: Can't We All Just Get Along?; Youth Issues, Youth Voices; and Towards a More Perfect Union. P.O. Box 203, Pomfret, CT, 06258. 860/928-2616.

Teaching Tolerance. Teaching Tolerance is a national education project dedicated to helping teachers foster equity, respect, and understanding in the classroom and beyond. A project of the Southern Poverty Law Center, Teaching Tolerance offers free or low-cost resources to educators at all levels, including the free video-and-text teaching kits, America s Civil Rights Movement and The Shadow o Hate, and Starting Small, a teacher-training kit for early childhood educators. The organization also publishes the free, semi-annual magazine Teaching Tolerance, which addresses classroom themes of tolerance, respect, and community-building and is distributed to more than one-half million educators throughout the U.S. and in 70 other countries. 400 Washington Avenue, Montgomery, AL, 36104. 334/264-0286. Fax: 334/264-7310.

Web Pages

Government Sites - U.S. Department of Education: Office for Civil Rights
www.ed.gov/offices/OCR
Office of Elementary and Secondary Education, Safe and Drug-Free Schools Program
www.ed.gov/offices/OESE/SDFS
U.S. Department of justice: "Hateful Acts Hurt Kids"
www.usdoj.gov/kidspage
Federal Bureau of Investigation Hate Crimes Report
www.fbi.gov/ucr/hatecm.htm
Montgomery County, Maryland, Committee on Hate Violence
members.aol.com/OneMC4AII/ndx.html
Washington State Safe Schools Coalition
members.tripod.com/-claytoly/ssp-home
Non-Profit and Educational Sites Anti-Defamation League
www.adl.org
Facing History and Ourselves National Foundation
www.facing.org
Improving America's Schools Education Reform Institute: Creating A Better School Environment
www.ncbe.gwu.edu//iasconferences//institutes//environment
Institute on Race and Poverty: Center on Speech, Equity and Harm
www.umn.edu/irp
Not in Our Town
www.igc.org/an/niot/
Teaching Tolerance
www.splcenter.org/teachingtolerance.html

Bibliography

Curricula and Instructional Materials

"1997 Hate Crimes Laws." Anti-Defamation League (1997). 800/343-5540; 212/885-7591.

A Policymaker's Guide to Hate Crimes. Bureau of Justice Assistance, U.S. Department of Justice, Washington D.C. (March, 1997). 800/688-4252.

An American Testament: Letters to the Burned Churches. Includes discussion guide with activities suitable for elementary and secondary school students. Anti-Defamation League (1996). 800/343-5540; 212/885-7591.

Facing History and Ourselves. Suitable for grades 7-12. Facing History and Ourselves National Foundation, Inc., Brookline, MA (1995). 617/232-1595.

Flirting or Hurting? A Teacher's Guide on Student-to-Student Sexual Harassment. Suitable for grades 6-12. Wellesley College Center for Women, Wellesley, MA (1994). 617/283-2510.

Hands Across Campus. Suitable for grades 6-12. American Jewish Committee, Washington DC (1996). 202/785-4200.

Hate Crime: A Sourcebook for Schools Confronting Bigotry, Harassment, Vandalism, and Violence. Bodingerdelbriarte, Christina and Sancho, Anthony. Philadelphia: Research for Better Schools (1992). Southwest Regional Laboratory. 562/598-7661.

Hate Crime: The Violence of Intolerance. U.S. Department of Justice, Community Relations Service, Washington, D.C. (1997). 202/305-2935.

Healing the Hate: A National Bias Crime Prevention Curriculum for Middle Schools. Suitable for grades 7-12. Office of Juvenile Justice and Delinquency Prevention, Washington D.C. (January, 1997). 800/638-8736.

PEARLS (People Empowered to Address Real Life Situations): Violence Prevention and Victim Assistance for Adolescents. Suitable for grades 8-12. Victim Services, New York, NY (1992). 718/624-2066.

Prejudice Reduction and Hate Crimes Prevention: An Annotated Bibliography of Resources for Teachers and School Administrators. New Jersey Department of Education, Division of Student Services, Office of Bilingual Education and Equity Issues. (August, 1997). 609/292-8777.

Pride in Who We Are: Compendium of Model Programs. New Jersey Department of Education, Division of Student Services, Office of Bilingual Education and Equity Issues (1997). 609/373-4089.

Project TEAMWORK-Athletes Against Violence Initiative: Empowering Students to More Effectively Deal with Racism, Prejudice, Bias and Conflict. Suitable for grades 6-12. Northeastern University's Center for the Study of Sport in Society, Boston, MA. 617/373-4025/4566.

Starting Small: Teaching Tolerance in Preschool and the Early Grades. Teaching Tolerance, Montgomery, AL. 334/264-7310.

Stop the Hate: A Community Brochure. El Hogar de la Paz. Tucson Police Dept., Pima County/Tucson AntiHate Crimes Task Force, Tucson Unified School District (1997). 520/791-4444.

Talking to Our Children About Racism, Prejudice, and Diversity. Suitable for grades K-3. Leadership Conference Education Fund, 1629 K Street, NW, Suite 1010, Washington D.C., 20006. 202/466-3434.

"Teacher They Called Me A ______!" Suitable for grades K-6. Anti-Defamation League, Hohokus, NJ. 800/343-5540.

Teaching Tolerance Magazine. Free semiannual magazine. Teachers and other educators can subscribe free of charge using official school letterhead. Teaching Tolerance, Montgomery, AL. 334/264-7310.

The Prejudice Book. Suitable for grades K-6. AntiDefamation League, Hohokus, NJ. 800/343-5540.

Tolerance for Diversity of Beliefs: A Secondary Curriculum Unit. Social Science Education Consortium, Boulder, CO. Suitable for grades 8-12. 303/492-8154.

WE: Lessons on Equal Worth and Dignity, the United Nations and Human Rights. Elliott, RoAnne and Simon, Ken. United Nations Association of the United States, Minneapolis, MN (1992). Suitable for grades 4-9.612/473-7813.

BOOKS

Ethnic Conflicts in Schools. Banfield, S. Springfield, NJ: Enslow Books (1995).

Facing Racial and Cultural Conflicts: Tools For Rebuilding Community. Washington D.C.: Program for Community Problems (1992).

Hate Crimes: The Rising Tide of Bigotry and Bloodshed. Levin, J., and McDevitt, J. New York: Plenum Press (1993).

It's Our World, Too: Stories of Young People Who Are Making A Difference. Hoose, Phillip. New York: Little, Brown and Co. (1993).

Multicultural Education in a Pluralistic Society. Gollnick, D.M., and Chinn, P.C. Columbus, OH: Merrill (1990).

Multiethnic Education: Theory and Practice. Banks, J.A. Needham Heights, MA: Allyn and Bacon (1988)

Perpetrators, Victims, Bystanders. Hilberg, Raul. Harper Collins (1992).

Preventing Prejudice: A Guide for Counselors and Educators. Ponterotto, G.J. and Pederson, B.P. Newbury Park, CA: Sage Publications (1993).

The Hate Crime. Karas, P. New York: Avon Books (1995).

The White Power Movement: America's Racist Hate Groups. Landau, E. Brookfield, CT: Millbrook Press.

Videos

Suitable for elementary school:

Starting Small. A video-and-text teacher training kit including exemplary tolerance education programs for use by early childhood educators. Free, one per school upon written request on letterhead from an elementary principal, day care director, or teacher education department chairperson. 58 Minutes. Teaching Tolerance, 400 Washington Avenue, Montgomery, AL, 36104. 334/264-0286. Fax: 334/264-7310.

Suitable for middle school and high school:

Babakiueria. A satire in which the roles of blacks and whites are reversed. A fleet of black settlers arrive to colonize an area inhabited by white natives. Designed to foster empathy. International. 30 Minutes. Landmark Films, Inc., 3450 Slade Run Drive, Falls Church, VA, 22042. 800/342-4336.

Names Can Really Hurt Us. A series of vignettes in which high school students describe hurtful incidents of prejudice and discrimination. Anti-Defamation League Materials Library, 22-D Hollywood Ave., Hohokus, NJ, 07423. 800/343-5540.

Not in Our Town. Award-winning PBS documentary showing how the town of Billings, Montana responded to an anti-Semitic hate incident with a community-wide show of support for the intended victims. The

Working Group, 5867 Ocean View Drive, Oakland, CA, 94618. 510/268-9675, ext. 317.

The Shadow of Hate. A video-and-classroom guide for secondary students. This Academy Award-nominated documentary traces the history of violence and prejudice in U.S. history against various racial and ethnic groups and women. Free, one per school upon written request on letterhead from a principal, university department, or community organization. 40 Minutes. Teaching Tolerance, 400 Washington Avenue, Montgomery, AL, 36104. 334/264-7310.

Skin. A dramatization of real life incidents, showing the problems minority teenagers encounter in their relationships with teachers, other students, and employers, because of their race or ethnicity. Landmark Films, Inc., 3450 Slade Run Drive, Falls Church, VA, 22042. 800/342-4336.

Skin Deep. Chronicles the experiences of a diverse and divided group of college freshmen as they explore their prejudices and try to understand each other's racial attitudes. California Newsreel, 149 Ninth Street, #420, San Francisco, CA, 94103. 415/621-6196.

Suspect. An African American businessman's encounter with a Latino cab driver who is reluctant to take him to his home in Harlem reveals prejudice and perceptions between minorities. Landmark Films, Inc., 3450 Slade Run Drive, Falls Church, VA, 22042. 800/342-4336.

A Time for Justice. An Academy Award winning documentary that surveys the civil rights movement through historical footage. Video and classroom guide. 38 Minutes. Direct Cinema Limited, P.O. Box 10003, Santa Monica, CA, 90410-10003. 310/636-8200. Fax: 310/636-8228.

Trouble Behind. Addresses the underlying causes and persistence of racism in an American town. Free facilitator's guide available. 56 Minutes. California Newsreel, 149 Ninth Street, #420, San Francisco, CA. 94103. 415/621-6196.

The full text of this public domain publication is available at the U.S. Department of Education's Safe and Drug-Free Schools Program home page at www.ed.gov/offices/OESE/SDFS, and at the U.S. Department of Justice's home page at www.usdoj.gov/topical.htm]. The text is also available in alternate formats upon request. For more information, please contact us at: U.S. Department of Education

Office of Elementary and Secondary Education Safe and Drug-Free Schools Program 600 Independence Avenue, SW Washington, D.C. 20202-6123; E-mail: SAFESCHL@ed.gov; Telephone: (202) 260-3954; TDD: 1-800-877-8339, 8 a.m. - 8 p.m., ET, M-F

In: School Crime and Safety ISBN 1-59454-736-X
Editor: Peter W. Amherst, pp. 23-38

Chapter 2

CRIME AND SAFETY IN AMERICA'S PUBLIC SCHOOLS: SELECTED FINDINGS FROM THE SCHOOL SURVEY ON CRIME AND SAFETY*

U.S. Department of Education and the National Center for Education Statistics

ABSTRACT

This chapter summarizes important findings from the 1999–2000 School Survey on Crime and Safety (SSOCS). This document presents selected national estimates of the amount of crime, violence, and disorder at public schools, and the practices and programs that schools use to identify and diffuse potential problems. Much of this document was adapted from analyses that were presented in two NCES publications, *Violence in U.S. Public Schools: 2000 School Survey on Crime and Safety* (2004–314) or *Indicators of School Crime and Safety: 2003* (2004–004).

* Excerpted from NCES 2004-370.

INTRODUCTION

Data on crime, violence, and disorder in our nation's schools are collected so that policymakers, parents, and educators will have information to identify emerging problems, and gauge the safety of American schools. Information on crime, violence, and disorder was collected in the 2000 SSOCS, a survey of public schools in the United States, sponsored by the National Center for Education Statistics (NCES). The 2000 SSOCS was a nationally representative sample of 2,270 regular public elementary, middle, secondary, and combined schools in the United States. Data from SSOCS helps to provide an overall picture of school crime and safety in the United States, by asking school principals about characteristics of school policies, school violence prevention programs and practices, violent deaths at school and elsewhere, frequency of crime and violence, disciplinary problems and actions, and school characteristics that have been associated with school crime.

SSOCS data are published in a variety of reports. For more information about the survey, go to the SSOCS web site (*http://nces.ed.gov/surveys/ssocs/*) to find an overview, questionnaires, and reports that can be viewed or downloaded.

CRIME AND VIOLENCE AT SCHOOL

Schools are entrusted with ensuring the safety of students *S*and staff. One measure of the safety of America's public schools is the presence of violence on school campuses. Public school principals were presented with a list of crimes and asked to report the total number of incidents of each crime for the 1999–2000 school year, as well as the number of crimes that were reported to police or other law enforcement personnel. A subset of crimes collected in SSOCS were those that were violent in nature. These violent incidents included rape, sexual battery other than rape, physical attacks or fights with and without a weapon, threats of physical attack with and without a weapon, and robberies with and without a weapon. In order to provide a measure of the most severe incidents, those crimes that would be considered aggravated assaults were included as serious violent incidents. Serious violent incidents included rape, sexual battery other than rape, physical attacks or fights with a weapon, threats of physical attack with a weapon, and robberies either with or without a weapon.

In 1999–2000, 71 percent of public elementary and secondary schools experienced at least one violent incident (figure 1). Approximately 1.5 million violent incidents occurred in about 59,000 public schools that year. Thirty-six percent of public schools reported at least one violent incident to police or other law enforcement personnel during the 1999–2000 school year (figure 2). Of the 1.5 million violent incidents that occurred at school, around 257,000 were reported to the police.

The most serious violence was experienced by a smaller percentage of schools. Twenty percent of public schools experienced at least one serious violent incident (including rape, sexual battery other than rape, physical attacks or fights with a weapon, threats of physical attack with a weapon, and robberies either with or without a weapon), for a total of 61,000 serious violent incidents (figure 1). Schools experiencing serious violence were likely to involve police. The majority of those schools that experienced a serious violent incident reported at least one of those incidents to the police or law enforcement personnel (figure 2). Specifically, of the 20 percent of schools with at least one serious violent incident, 15 percent of schools reported a serious violent incident to the police. This means 75 percent of schools that had a serious violent incident reported at least one of those incidents to the authorities.

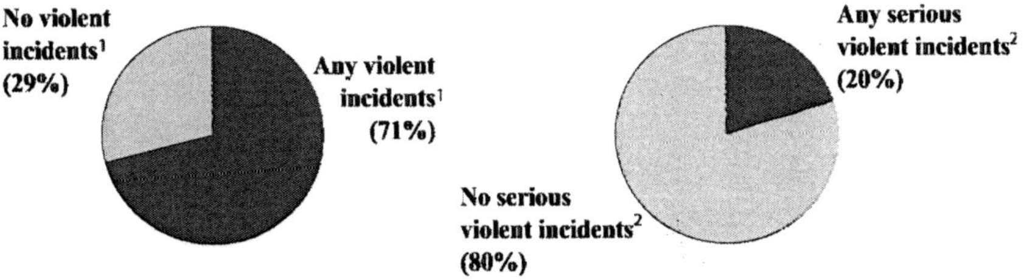

Figure 1. Percentage of public schools that experienced violent and serious violent incidents: 1999–2000

[1] Violent incidents include rape, sexual battery other than rape, physical attack or fight with or without a weapon, threat of physical attack with or without a weapon, and robbery with or without a weapon.

[2] Serious violent incidents include rape, sexual battery other than rape, physical attack or fight with a weapon, threat of physical attack with a weapon, and robbery with or without a weapon.

Source: U.S. Department of Education, National Center for Education Statistics, School Survey on Crime and Safety (SSOCS), 2000. (Estimates previously published in tables 1 and 2 of Violence in U.S. Public Schools: 2000 School Survey on Crime and Safety [NCES 2004–314].)

The 2000 SSOCS asked principals about a variety of crimes in addition to those that were violent. In 1999–2000, schools were more likely to have experienced at least one physical attack or fight without a weapon than any other type of crime (64 percent) (figure 3). Threats of physical attack without a weapon (52 percent) and vandalism (51 percent) were the second most reported crimes during 1999–2000, followed by theft or larceny (46 percent), and possession of a knife or sharp object (43 percent). Of those crimes presented to principals, sexual battery other than rape (2 percent), rape or attempted rape (1 percent), and robbery with a weapon (0 percent) were least likely to occur at school.

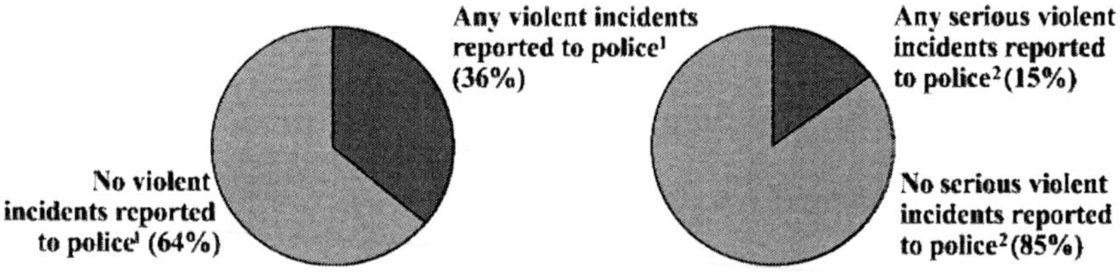

Figure 2. Percentage of public schools that reported violent and serious violent incidents to police: 1999–2000

[1] Violent incidents include rape, sexual battery other than rape, physical attack or fight with or without a weapon, threat of physical attack with or without a weapon, and robbery with or without a weapon.

[2] Serious violent incidents include rape, sexual battery other than rape, physical attack or fight with a weapon, threat of physical attack with a weapon, and robbery with or without a weapon.

Source: U.S. Department of Education, National Center for Education Statistics, School Survey on Crime and Safety (SSOCS), 2000. (Estimates previously published in tables 1 and 2 of Violence in U.S. Public Schools: 2000 School Survey on Crime and Safety [NCES 2004-314].)

Figure 3. Percentage of public schools with specific crimes: 1999–2000
Source: U.S. Department of Education, National Center for Education Statistics, School Survey on Crime and Safety (SSOCS), 2000. (Estimates previously published in tables 3, 4, 5, and 6 of Violence in U.S. Public Schools: 2000 School Survey on Crime and Safety [NCES 2004–314].)

DISORDER

Disciplinary problems in school can lead to school disorder that distracts from the ability of teachers to teach and students to learn. A selection of discipline problems were included in the 1999–2000 SSOCS, and principals were asked to report with what frequency those problems occurred at school. The discipline problems included student racial tensions, student bullying, student verbal abuse of teachers, widespread disorder in classrooms, student acts of disrespect for teachers, undesirable gang activities, and undesirable cult or extremist group activities. The level of frequency that a principal reported was used to determine whether the school had a serious problem. Student racial tensions, student bullying, student verbal abuse of teachers, widespread disorder in classrooms, and student acts of disrespect for teachers were considered a serious discipline problem if they were reported to occur daily or weekly. Undesirable gang and cult or extremist group activities were considered a serious discipline problem if they happened at all during the school year.

In 1999–2000, schools were more likely to have a serious problem with student bullying than with any other discipline problem (29 percent). Student acts of disrespect for teachers and undesirable gang activities (19 percent each) were the second most reported serious problems for public schools.

Among the other discipline problems reported, 13 percent of schools reported student verbal abuse of teachers, 7 percent of schools reported undesirable cult or extremist group activities, and 3 percent of schools reported student racial tensions and widespread disorder in classrooms.

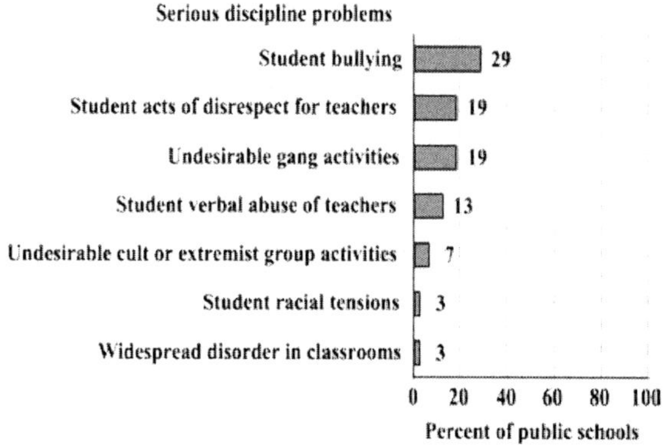

Figure 4. Percentage of public schools that reported selected discipline problems at school as serious: 1999–2000

Source: U.S. Department of Education, National Center for Education Statistics, School Survey on Crime and Safety (SSOCS), 2000. (Estimates previously published in figure 16.1 of Indicators of School Crime and Safety: 2003 [NCES 2004–004].)

Disciplinary Actions

Principals were asked to report the number of disciplinary actions taken for specific offenses during the 1999–2000 school year. Serious disciplinary actions included suspensions lasting 5 days or more, removals from school with no continuing services (i.e., expulsions), and transfers to specialized schools. About 54 percent of public schools took a serious disciplinary action for any of the specified offenses that occurred in the 1999–2000 school year, for a total of about 1,163,000 actions. Of those serious disciplinary actions, 83 percent were suspensions (for 5 days or more), 11 percent were removals with no services, and 7 percent were transfers to specialized schools (figure 5).

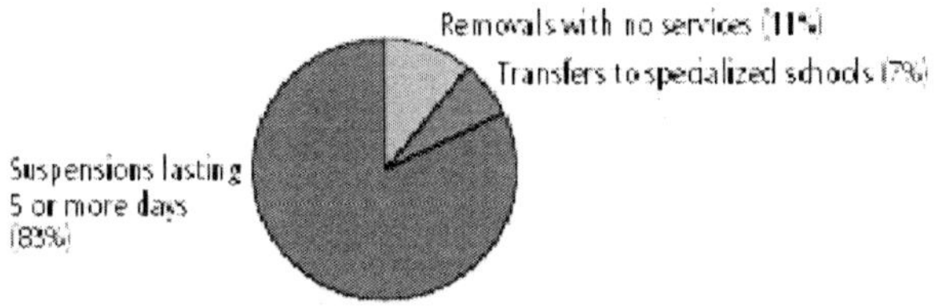

Figure 5. Percentage distribution of serious disciplinary actions taken by public school principals according to type of action: 1999–2000
Note: Detail may not sum to total because of rounding.
Source: U.S. Department of Education, National Center for Education Statistics, School Survey on Crime and Safety (SSOCS), 2000. (Estimates previously published in figure 8.1 of Indicators of School Crime and Safety: 2003 [NCES 2004–004].)

Two percent of all public schools took a serious disciplinary action for the use of a firearm or explosive device, and 4 percent did so for the possession of such a device. Use of weapons other than firearms resulted in a serious disciplinary action in 5 percent of schools, while possession of weapons other than firearms led to an action in 19 percent of schools.

Ten percent of all public schools took a serious disciplinary action for the distribution of illegal drugs, and 20 percent for the possession or use of illegal drugs or alcohol. In 1999–2000, public schools also reported other reasons for taking serious disciplinary actions in their schools, including fights (35 percent), threats (22 percent), insubordination (18 percent), and other infractions not including academic ones (14 percent).

Violence Prevention Programs for Students

One approach to reducing the level of crime and violence in schools is to provide students with training intended to prevent certain behaviors. Principals were asked about specific components of formal student programs to prevent or reduce violence at their school. During the 1999–2000 school year, the most frequently reported program components were counseling, social work, psychological, or therapeutic activity (66 percent); behavioral or behavior modification intervention (66 percent); prevention curriculum, instruction, or training (65 percent); and individual attention, mentoring, tutoring, or coaching by students or adults (63 percent) (figure 6). Over half of schools (57 percent) reported the next most common program component, which was programs to promote a sense of community or social integration among students. The program component provided in the survey least reported by school principals was a hotline or tipline for students to report problems (22 percent).

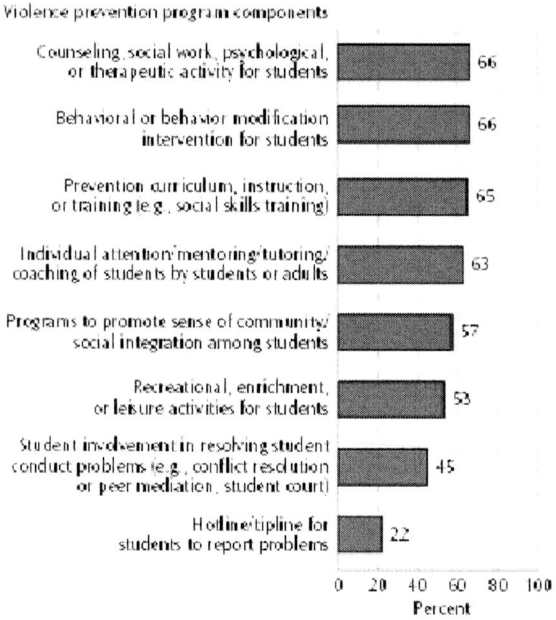

Figure 6. Percentage of public schools with specific violence prevention program components for students: 1999–2000

Source: U.S. Department of Education, National Center for Education Statistics, School Survey on Crime and Safety (SSOCS), 2000.

TEACHER AND PARENT INVOLVEMENT IN PREVENTION EFFORTS

Teachers

Another approach to crime and violence prevention that schools employed was to provide training to teachers and staff. Some types of teacher training included classroom management, crime prevention, and recognition of early warning signs of potentially violent students. In the

1999–2000 school year, 66 percent of schools reported that they trained, supervised, or offered technical assistance in classroom management for teachers, 35 percent trained teachers or aides to recognize early warning signs of potentially violent students, and 31 percent trained faculty and staff in crime prevention (figure 7).

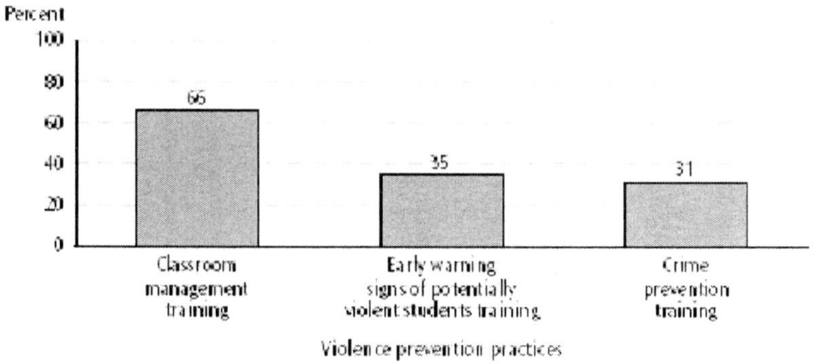

Figure 7. Percentage of public schools that train staff in specific violence prevention practices: 1999–2000

Source: U.S. Department of Education, National Center for Education Statistics, School Survey on Crime and Safety (SSOCS), 2000.

Parents

In addition to training students, teachers, and staff about violence prevention, many schools involved parents in crime reduction efforts. Schools may seek feedback from parents on school policies or formalize programs or training in issues related to school disorder. During 1999–2000, schools were more likely to obtain input from parents about policies related to school crime and discipline (54 percent) than either to offer training or technical assistance to parents in dealing with students' problem behavior (45 percent), or to have a program that involved parents at school helping to maintain discipline (21 percent) (figure 8).

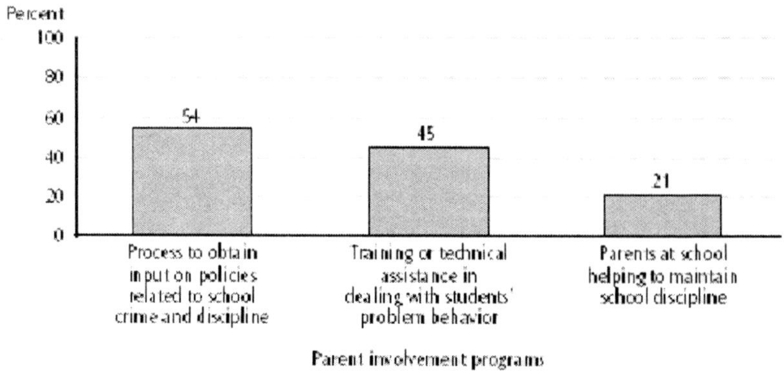

Figure 8. Percentage of public schools with selected parent involvement programs: 1999–2000

Source: U.S. Department of Education, National Center for Education Statistics, School Survey on Crime and Safety (SSOCS), 2000.

CRIME AND SAFETY PRACTICES

Schools typically employ specific practices and procedures designed to ensure the safety of the students and staff. Some of these practices are intended to limit the access that people have to school campuses, while other practices monitor people's behavior once they are on campus. SSOCS asked principals about a variety of practices that schools utilized during the 1999–2000 school year. Figure 9 shows those practices that schools used to limit access to school campuses. The vast majority of public schools required visitors to sign or check in when entering the school building (97 percent), while few schools required that either students or visitors pass through metal detectors (1 percent).

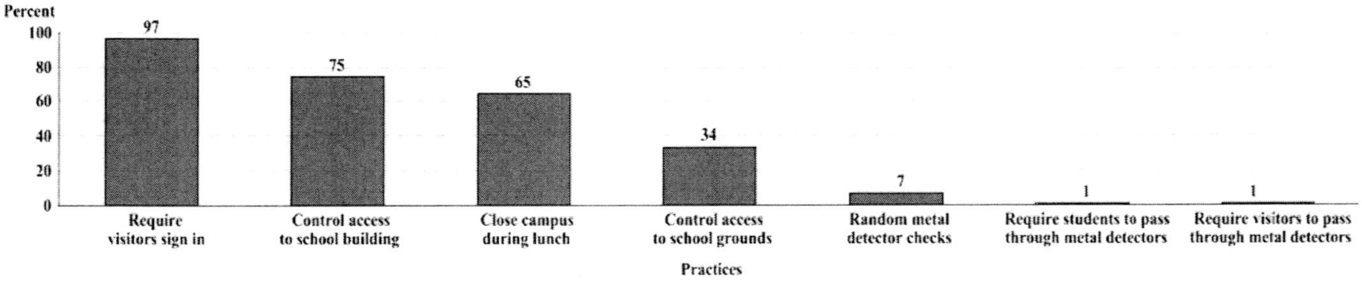

Figure 9. Percentage of public schools that limit access to campus with selected practices: 1999–2000

Source: U.S. Department of Education, National Center for Education Statistics, School Survey on Crime and Safety (SSOCS), 2000.

Schools use different security measures to monitor the activities of those within the school building. Some of these security measures may include using technology to monitor the school grounds, searching or testing for drugs, or limiting the amount of space available for concealing weapons or drugs. In 1999–2000, schools used a variety of practices to prevent or reduce specific behaviors. Schools were more likely not to provide lockers to students than any other practice used to monitor activities (54 percent) (figure 10). A similar practice is for schools to require clear book bags or ban book bags entirely, which was used by fewer schools (6 percent). While 25 percent of schools required faculty or staff to wear picture IDs, only 4 percent of schools had the same requirement for students. In order to reduce the presence of drugs at school, 21 percent of schools used random dog sniffs, 12 percent of schools had random sweeps for contraband, and 4 percent of schools required drug testing for any students. Finally, 19 percent of schools used security cameras to monitor the school.

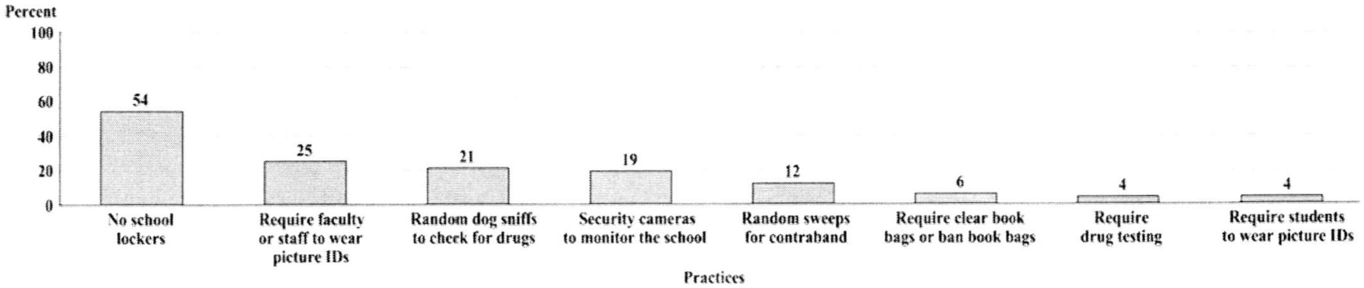

Figure 10. Percentage of public schools that monitor campus with selected practices: 1999–2000

Source: U.S. Department of Education, National Center for Education Statistics, School Survey on Crime and Safety (SSOCS), 2000.

Crisis Management Plans

It is important that schools are prepared to respond in the event of a crisis. One action taken by schools is to have a written plan that details the procedures that are to be performed in the event of a crisis. During the 1999–2000 school year, 96 percent of schools had a written plan for at least one of the following crises: shootings, riots or large-scale fights, schoolwide threats such as bomb or anthrax scares, natural disasters, or hostages. Schools were more likely to have a written plan for natural disasters (92 percent) and bomb scares, anthrax scares, or comparable schoolwide threats (91 percent) than other types of crises (figure 11). In addition, more than half of schools had a written plan for shootings (74 percent), hostages (67 percent), and riots or large-scale fights (61 percent).

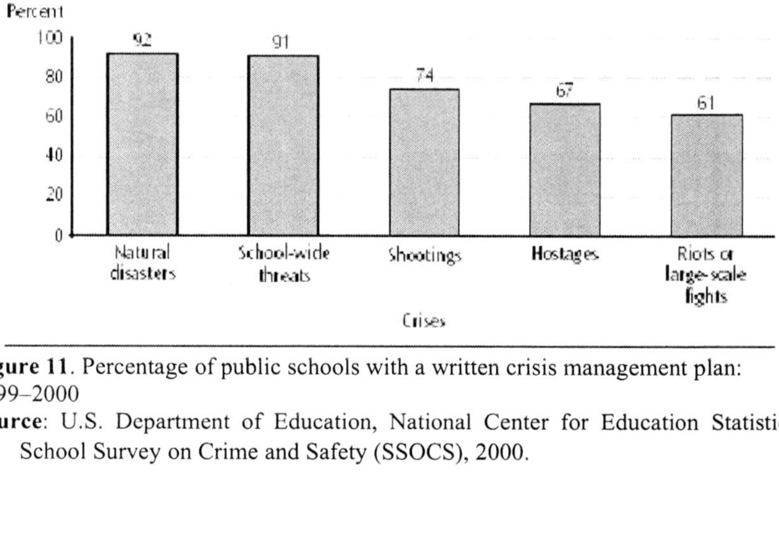

Figure 11. Percentage of public schools with a written crisis management plan: 1999–2000

Source: U.S. Department of Education, National Center for Education Statistics, School Survey on Crime and Safety (SSOCS), 2000.

Barriers to Safe Schools

While programs and policies may help in reducing crime and violence in schools, some factors serve as limitations to crime reduction or prevention efforts. In 1999–2000, principals reported that a wide variety of factors limited their schools' efforts to reduce or prevent crime. Among those limiting factors, principals were most likely to report the lack of alternative placements or programs for disruptive students as a limitation to reducing or preventing crime (67 percent) (figure 12). Inadequate funding (62 percent) and federal policies on disciplining disabled students (60 percent) were the second most frequently reported limitations by school principals, followed by the lack of or inadequate teacher training in classroom management (50 percent). A lack of teacher support for school policies (19 percent) and a fear of district or state reprisal (19 percent) were reported as limitations by the fewest principals.

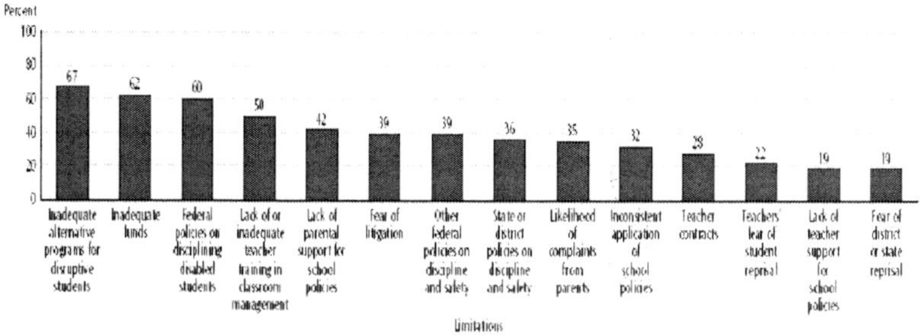

Figure 12. Percentage of public schools that reported that specific factors limited their ability to reduce or prevent crime: 1999–2000

Source: U.S. Department of Education, National Center for Education Statistics, School Survey on Crime and Safety (SSOCS), 2000.

Frequently Asked Questions about SSOCS

The School Survey on Crime and Safety (SSOCS) is the National Center for Education Statistics' sample survey of the nation's public schools designed to provide estimates of school crime, discipline, disorder, and programs and policies related to crime and disorder. SSOCS is administered to public elementary, middle, secondary, and combined school principals during the Spring of a school year.

Who Participates in SSOCS?

Over 3,000 public school principals are selected to receive the SSOCS questionnaire. The SSOCS sample is large enough to provide national estimates of all public schools, while taking into account the level of instruction, type of location, and size of the student enrollment.

When is SSOCS Administered?

SSOCS is administered at the end of the school year to allow principals to report the most complete information possible. SSOCS was first administered to principals in April of the 1999–2000 school year. The next administration of SSOCS will be in the Spring of the 2003–04 school year.

What Topics are Covered by SSOCS?

The SSOCS questionnaire asks principals to report on a variety of topics related to crime and safety, including the following:

- Characteristics of school policies and procedures,
- School violence prevention programs and practices,
- Use of law enforcement personnel or security services,
- Frequency of criminal incidents at school,
- Frequency of incidents reported to police or law enforcement,
- Frequency of hate-related and gang-related incidents,
- Disciplinary problems and disciplinary actions, and
- Other school characteristics related to school crime.

Where Can I Learn More about SSOCS and other Crime and Safety Data Collections?

SSOCS data are published in a variety of reports. For more information about the survey, go to the SSOCS web site (*http://nces.ed.gov/ssoc*s) to find an overview, questionnaires, and reports that can be viewed or downloaded.

While SSOCS collects information from school principals, NCES also administers surveys to students, teachers, and parents. Information about SSOCS and other NCES school crime surveys can be found at *http://nces.ed.gov/programs/crime*.

In: School Crime and Safety ISBN 1-59454-736-X
Editor: Peter W. Amherst, pp. 39-97

Chapter 3

STUDENT REPORTS OF BULLYING: RESULTS FROM THE 2001 SCHOOL CRIME SUPPLEMENT TO THE NATIONAL CRIME VICTIMIZATION SURVEY*

Jill F. DeVoe and Sarah Kaffenberger

ABSTRACT

Bullying in schools is an issue that continues to receive attention from researchers, educators, parents, and students. Despite the common assumption that bullying is a normal part of childhood and encompasses minor teasing and harassment (Lawrence 1998), researchers increasingly find that bullying is a problem that can be detrimental to students' well-being (Nansel et al. 2001, 2003; Haynie et al. 2001).

Bullying is commonly defined as being "exposed, repeatedly and over time, to negative actions on the part of one or more other students" (Olweus 1991). Olweus also suggests that bullying can be characterized by two distinct forms of negative actions: direct and indirect bullying behaviors. Direct bullying takes the form of overt, physical contact in which the victim is openly attacked. Indirect bullying takes the form of social isolation and intentional exclusion

---

* Excerpted from NCES 2005-310, dated July 2005.

from activities. Both forms of bullying, occurring separately or together, can be harmful to students' well-being and development.

This chapter examines the prevalence and nature of bullying in relation to student characteristics, school characteristics, and victimization. In addition, the study explores other behaviors that were reported by the victim, such as fear, avoidance behavior, weapon carrying, and academic grades. It also examines student reports of being bullied by direct means only, bullied by indirect means only, and bullied both directly and indirectly. Readers are alerted to the limitations of the survey design and analysis approach with regard to causality. Conclusions about causality can not be made due to the cross-sectional, nonexperimental design of the survey used. And, while certain characteristics discussed in this chapter, such as school control, gang presence, security guards, and hallway monitors, may be related to one another, this analysis does not control for such relationships. Therefore, no causal inferences should be made between the variables of interest and bullying when reading these results.

As reported by public and private school students, ages 12 through 18, in the 2001 School Crime Supplement (SCS) to the National Crime Victimization Survey (NCVS), major findings include the following:

- **Fourteen percent of students reported being the victims of bullying.** In 2001, 14 percent of students ages 12 through 18 reported that they had been bullied at school in the 6 months prior to the interview (appendix B, table 1). About 3 percent reported that they had been bullied only through direct or physical means, almost 7 percent reported being bullied only indirectly through social exclusion or rejection, and approximately 5 percent reported being bullied both directly and indirectly.[1]
- **Sex differences were not detected in most types of bullying.** No measurable differences were detected between boys and girls in reports of being bullied, directly or indirectly, in the 6 months

[1] Youth ages 12 through 18 were first asked "Have you been bullied at school? That is, has anyone picked on you a lot or tried to make you do things you did not want to do (e.g., give them money)?" This is referred to as direct bullying. Students were also asked, "Have you felt rejected because other students have made fun of you, called you names, or excluded you from activities?" This is referred to as indirect bullying. References to "bullying" include youth who reported they were either directly or indirectly bullied. Categories are mutually exclusive. Directly Only, Indirectly Only, and Both Directly and Indirectly are distinct categories. Students appearing in one category do not appear in other categories.

prior to the survey (appendix B, table 1). However, differences did emerge between boys and girls who were bullied both directly and indirectly. Specifically, boys were more likely than girls to report being the victims of both direct and indirect bullying (5 percent of boys vs. 4 percent of girls).

- **White, non-Hispanic students were more likely than Black, non-Hispanic students and Other, non-Hispanic students to report being bullied**[2] (15 percent of White students vs. 12 percent and 11 percent of Other and Black students, respectively) (appendix B, table 1). When reports of indirect bullying only were examined, White students' and Black students' reports exceeded those of Hispanic students (7 percent, 7 percent, and 4 percent, respectively). White students (5 percent) were more likely than Black students (3 percent) to report being bullied both directly and indirectly.
- **Younger students were more likely than older students to report being bullied**. Students' reports of being bullied (either directly or indirectly) decreased as grade level increased from 6th (24 percent) to 12th grade (7 percent) (appendix B, table 1).
- **Differences were not detected between public and private school students' reports of being bullied at school.** No measurable differences were detected in public and private school students' reports of being bullied, directly or indirectly, or in both ways (appendix B, table 2).
- **Students in schools where gangs were present were more likely to report being the victims of bullying.** In 2001, students who reported the presence of street gangs at school were more likely to report being bullied (21 percent) than those who reported no presence of street gangs (13 percent) (appendix B, table 2).
- **Fewer students reported bullying in schools with supervision by police officers, security officers, or staff hallway monitors.** In schools where a security guard or assigned police officer was present, fewer students (13 percent) reported being bullied compared to students in schools with no such supervision (16 percent) (appendix B, table 2). Fewer students in schools with staff hallway monitors reported being bullied than did students in schools without such hallway supervision (14 vs. 18 percent).
- **Victims of bullying were more likely to experience a criminal victimization at school.** Bullied students were more likely to experience any type of victimization (13 percent), a serious violent victimization (2 percent), a violent victimization (7 percent), or a

[2] For ease of presentation, White, non-Hispanic, Black, non-Hispanic, and Other, non-Hispanic race/ethnicities will be described as White, Black, and Other.

property victimization (8 percent) at school when compared to those students who were not bullied (4 percent, 0.3 percent, 1 percent, and 4 percent, respectively) (appendix B, table 3).[3] Students who reported only direct bullying were more likely to be violently victimized than students who reported only indirect bullying (11 percent vs. 3 percent).

- **Victims of bullying were more afraid of being attacked at school and elsewhere.** Bullied students were more likely to report being fearful of attack at school at least some of the time (18 percent), on the way to and from school (11 percent), and away from school (12 percent) than were students who were not bullied (3 percent, 2 percent, and 3 percent, respectively) (appendix B, table 4).
- **Victims of bullying were more likely to avoid certain areas of the school and certain activities out of fear of an attack.** Specifically, bullied students were more likely than nonbullied students to report the following avoidance behaviors: avoiding the shortest route to school (6 percent of bullied students vs. 2 percent of nonbullied students); the entrance to the school (4 percent vs. 1 percent); hallways or stairs (7 percent vs. 1 percent); and the school cafeteria (6 percent vs. 1 percent) (appendix B, table 5). Bullied students were also more likely than nonbullied students to avoid restrooms (7 percent vs. 2 percent), the parking lot (5 percent vs. 1 percent), and other places inside the school building (5 percent vs. 1 percent) or other places on school grounds (6 percent vs. 1 percent).
- **Victims of bullying were more likely to report that they carried weapons to school and were engaged in physical fights.** Specifically, students who were bullied were more likely to report that they carried a weapon to school for protection (4 percent), as compared to students who were not bullied (1 percent) (appendix B, table 6). Bullied students were also more likely to report being involved in a physical fight (15 percent), compared to nonbullied students (4 percent).
- **Of those students who reported lower grades, victims of bullying were more likely to report receiving D's and F's than their nonbullied counterparts.** Bullied students were more likely to report receiving lower academic grades, or mostly D's and F's, than their nonbullied peers (8 percent vs. 3 percent) (appendix B, table 7). Victims of both forms of bullying were more likely to report

[3] Serious violent crimes include rape, sexual assault, robbery, and aggravated assault. Violent crimes include serious violent crimes and simple assault. Any crimes include violent crimes and theft.

mostly D's and F's (12 percent) than those bullied either directly only or indirectly only (7 percent and 6 percent).

INTRODUCTION

Students are victims of a spectrum of problem behaviors at school, ranging from minor disciplinary problems to criminal victimization (DeVoe et al. 2004). Bullying is one form of these problem behaviors that concerns students, educators, and parents because of its potential detriment to the students' well-being (Nansel et al. 2001, 2003; Haynie et al. 2001).

Defining bullying is a difficult task; however, most research agrees that bullying comprises physical, verbal, and psychological behaviors such as hitting, teasing, taunting, and manipulating social relationships (Banks 1997; Ericson 2001). The investigation of bullying is further complicated by the complex dynamics of bullying scenarios and the developmental context for social development in which bullying plays a role. Further, aggression among youth often serves varied purposes for children at different stages of development.

Hawkins, Pepler, and Craig (2001) found that peers were present in 88 percent of bullying episodes. Thus, bullying frequently involves the support of peers within the school community and is often not an isolated event between two individuals. In addition, aggressive behavior, such as bullying, is expressed differently over time and may change in purpose, as children transition from middle to secondary school. As Cairns et al. (1989) discuss, patterns of, and motivation for aggression change over the course of childhood and cannot be examined independently of the developmental context in which aggression occurs. Cillessen and Mayeaux (2004) found that physical and relational aggression, peer approval, and popularity were intricately linked, but that the relationships between these variables vary with age, gender, and by type of aggression. While resolution to these definitional, contextual, and developmental complexities are unable to be addressed in the current investigation, this chapter provides a broad summary of bullying reported by student victims in 2001.

Olweus (1993) has produced an instructive definition of bullying that includes three essential elements of bullying behavior: (1) the behavior is aggressive and negative; (2) the behavior is carried out repeatedly; and (3) the behavior occurs in a relationship where there is an imbalance of power between the parties involved. This tripartite definition of bullying is now used by many researchers (e.g., Smith et al. 2002). In a further refinement of the variety of behaviors that encompass bullying, Olweus identifies two subtypes of bullying that are used as the basis of this chapter. The first subtype is direct, physical aggression, and the second is indirect behavior such as social exclusion or rejection. Direct bullying often takes the form of overt, physical contact in which the victim is openly attacked. Indirect bullying often takes the form of social isolation and intentional exclusion from activities. Research suggests that indirect forms of bullying are more often employed by girls than boys (Ericson 2001; Banks 1997; Carney and Merrell 2001; Crick and Grotpeter 1995). Researchers of aggression stress the importance of the distinction between its physical and social forms. Underwood, Galen, and Paquette (2001) more recently coined the term "social aggression" to encompass the less physical and indirect forms of hurtful behavior. These authors discourage the use of the term "indirect" because the term implies that the behavior does not involve direct or overt interaction with the victim. They also favor the term "social aggression" as it more aptly targets the purpose of the behavior as harmful. Finally, they believe that this type of aggression can be conveyed through nonverbal means, such as social exclusion and the term "social aggression" is more accurate.

For the purposes of this article, the term "indirect" will be retained to show the dichotomy of behaviors being discussed and to maintain the conceptualization proposed by Olweus, recognizing that more current conceptualizations exist in the literature. The term "indirect bullying" includes both verbal and nonverbal behaviors, and does not imply that the victim was unaware of the activity.

This Statistical Analysis Report provides estimates of bullying at school as reported by students ages 12 through 18 who were enrolled in grades 6 through 12 in the 6 months prior to survey administration. School-related data are drawn from the 2001 School Crime Supplement (SCS) to the National Crime Victimization Survey (NCVS). Data about characteristics of the individual (including sex, race/ethnicity, household income, and urbanicity) and victimization are drawn from NCVS variables appended to the SCS data.

The NCVS is the nation's primary source of information on crime victimization and the victims of crime. The NCVS collects detailed information on the frequency and nature of crimes experienced by Americans and their households each year. The survey measures both crimes reported and not reported to police. The NCVS collects data on all members of selected households and surveys all who are age 12 and above, for a total of about 79,000 people, every 6 months.

The SCS is a supplement to the NCVS that was created to collect additional information about school-related victimization on a national level. It is administered for a 6-month period from January through June in all NCVS households. The SCS is a nationally representative sample of students ages 12 through 18 and has been administered in 1989, 1995, 1999, 2001, and 2003, with plans for collection in 2005. This study focuses on the 2001 collection. Respondents eligible for the supplement were those in the specified age range who attended school during the 6 months prior to the interview and were enrolled in grades 6 through 12. A total of 8,374 students participated in the 2001 SCS.

The 2001 SCS questionnaire measures respondents' perceptions of whether they have been bullied directly and/or indirectly, and specifies the aggressive nature of the behavior and whether or not the behavior happens "often" or "a lot." Specifically, youth were first asked "Have you been bullied at school? That is, has anyone picked on you a lot or tried to make you do things you did not want to do (e.g., give them money)?" This is referred to as *direct* bullying. In a separate question, students were also asked if they have often felt rejected by other students at school: "Have you felt rejected because other students have made fun of you, called you names, or excluded you from activities?" This type of bullying is referred to as *indirect* bullying.

This chapter focuses not only on the prevalence of bullying, but also on those subsets of students who reported being the victims of direct bullying, indirect bullying, and both direct and indirect bullying. Different types of bullying may affect different groups of students, occur in different types of schools, or affect student behavior in different ways. These distinctions allow readers to differentiate between students who were either physically (directly) *or* socially (indirectly) bullied, and also to identify those students who were bullied *both* physically and socially.[4] Additional analysis describes the characteristics of students affected by these types of behavior and the characteristics of schools in which these behaviors occur. Because of prior research that suggests victims of bullying may resort to aggressive behaviors in response to being bullied (Nansel et al. 2003), the extent to which reports of bullying arerelated to victim behaviors such as weapon carrying, physical fights, fear, and avoidance is explored. Finally, for educators, the academic

---

[4] Students who reported being the victims of both forms of bullying were not necessarily bullied more than students who reported either direct or indirect bullying. Rather, these students simply reported that they were subject to a wider variety of bullying behaviors including both direct and indirect means.

success of students is of paramount importance. For this reason, self-reported academic performance of bullied students is also examined.

Readers should note that estimates of bullying presented in this study are derived from victims' self-reports of bullying experiences. Limitations inherent to victimization surveys such as the SCS might impact estimates of bullying (Cantor and Lynch 2000). First, the SCS includes unbounded interviews, or interviews that include victimizations that exceed the 6-month reference period asked of SCS respondents. This may artificially increase reports of victimization since respondents may recall events outside of the given reference period. Second, the SCS does not use a classification scheme for determining bullying events. That is, the larger NCVS uses sets of characteristics to classify events as criminal whereas the SCS often relies on the respondent to self-determine a condition. This allows for the victim to use his own interpretation or conceptions to define a situation, when the same situation may not have been labeled bullying by a bystander or the offender. Third, victim surveys emphasize crime events as incidents at one point in time. Reality tells us that victims can often live in a state of victimization where they are threatened or victimized regularly. While the NCVS does allow for these series to be flagged for criminal victimizations, reports of bullying behaviors are not collected in this way.

Additional caution is in order when examining bullying as well as the other variables used in this report. Because all variables of interest on the SCS are self-reported, information about the respondent and his school may be inaccurate due to error in recall, falsification, or exaggeration. For example, a student either may not be forthright or artificially inflate his self-reported academic grades. In addition, the respondent may forget a bullying event entirely or recall the characteristics of the event inaccurately. This would lead to an underestimation of victimization. There is no independent or external verification of any of the SCS variables used in this report.

Finally, readers are alerted to the limitations of the survey design and analysis approach with regard to causality. Conclusions about causality can not be made due to the cross-sectional, non-experimental design of the SCS. And, while certain characteristics discussed in this report, such as school control, gang presence, security guards and hallway monitors, may be related to one another, this analysis does not control for such relationships. Therefore, no causal inferences should be made between the variables of interest and bullying when reading these results.

PREVALENCE OF BULLYING IN SCHOOLS

In 2001, approximately 14 percent of students ages 12 through 18 were victims of bullying at school in the 6 months prior to the survey administration (figure 1 and appendix B, table 1). For this report, the total percentage of students bullied refers to those students who were either directly or indirectly bullied. Three percent reported only direct bullying—that someone had picked on them a lot or tried to make them do something they did not want to do. Seven percent of students reported only indirect bullying—that other students had rejected them or excluded them from activities. Five percent reported being bullied both directly and indirectly.

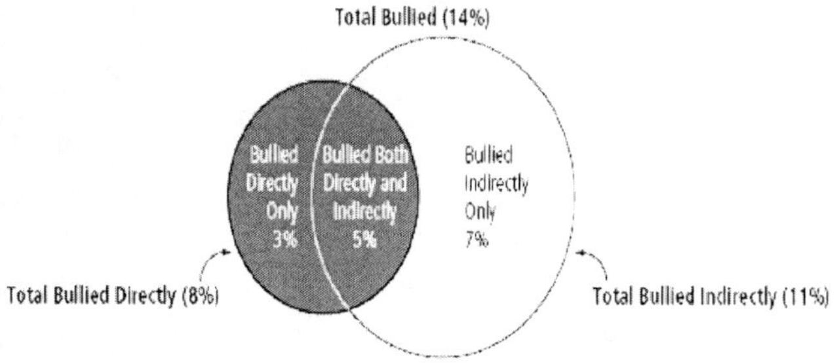

Figure 1. Percentage of students ages 12–18 who reported being bullied, bullied directly only, bullied indirectly only, and bullied in both ways: 2001

Note: "At school" was defined as in the school building, on school property, on a school bus, or going to and from school.Youth ages 12 through 18 were first asked if "they had been bullied at school. That is, had anyone picked on them a lot or tried to make them do things they did not want to do (e.g., give them money)?" This is referred to as direct bullying. They were also asked, "Have you felt rejected because other students have made fun of you, called you names, or excluded you from activities?"This is referred to as indirect bullying. Total includes youth who reported they were bullied directly or indirectly. Population size for students ages 12–18 is 24,315,000. Detail may not sum to total because of rounding.

Source: U.S. Department of Justice, Bureau of Justice Statistics, School Crime Supplement (SCS) to the National Crime Victimization Survey, 2001.

CHARACTERISTICS OF BULLIED STUDENTS

When looking at the direct and indirect forms of bullying, prior research suggests, first, that boys typically engage in more direct bullying methods than girls and are more often the victims of this type of bullying (Nansel et al. 2001; Olweus 1997). Second, research suggests indirect bullying, such as social exclusion and rejection, is the type of bullying used more frequently by girls than boys (Banks 1997; Olweus 1997, 1999). In this analysis of the 2001 SCS, no measurable differences were detected between boys and girls in their reports of direct or indirect bullying only, but when looking at students who were bullied *both* directly and indirectly, measurable differences did emerge (appendix B, table 1). In the 2001 SCS, boys were more likely than girls to report being both directly and indirectly bullied (5 percent of boys vs. 4 percent of girls) (appendix B, table 1).

White, non-Hispanic students were more likely than Other, non-Hispanic students and Black, non-Hispanic students to report being bullied (15 percent of White, non-Hispanic students vs. 11 percent and 12 percent of Other, non-Hispanic and Black, non-Hispanic students, respectively) (appendix B, table 1).[5] When indirect bullying behavior was examined, White and Black students' reports (7 percent each) were higher than those of Hispanic students' (4 percent). Those students who were bullied both directly and indirectly were more likely to be White than Black (5 percent vs. 3 percent).[6] No measurable - racial/ethnic differences in bullying were detected among victims of only direct bullying behavior. While the research on race/ethnicity and bullying is scant, the findings by Nansel et al. (2001) found that Black youth were less likely than their White and Hispanic peers to report being bullied.

As the grade levels of students in the 2001 SCS increased, from 6th through 12th grades, the total percentage of students reporting that they were bullied decreased (figure 2 and appendix B, table 1). Specifically, 24 percent of 6th-graders reported being bullied at school, compared to 7 percent of 12th-graders. Sixth-grade students were more likely than 12th-grade students to report both direct (5 percent vs. 1 percent) and indirect (10 percent vs. 5

---

[5] For the remainder of this report, White, non-Hispanic; Black, non-Hispanic; and Other, non-Hispanic race/ethnicities are described as White, Black, and Other, respectively, for ease of presentation.

[6] While estimates among other race/ethnicity categories may appear to be different, these differences may not be statistically significant due to large standard errors. Please refer to Appendix A for further discussion about standard errors and the design of the survey.

percent) bullying. This finding is consistent with previous research on bullying and grade level and is explained in terms of establishing social hierarchies. Specifically, prior researchers suggest that bullying may be used as a way to establish dominance in social structures and that the transition to middle school (which traditionally occurs around the 6th grade) should be accompanied by an increase in bullying and then follow an age-related decline as dominance hierarchies are solidified (Pellegrini and Long 2002; Pellegrini and Bartini 2001). Another possible reason for this finding comes from Olweus' (1993) research, which suggests that younger and weaker students are exposed more frequently to bullying and that a considerable part of bullying behavior is carried out by older students against these younger victims.

Olweus (1978, 1980) found no relationship between socioeconomic status of the family and being the victim of bullying and suggests that there are similar proportions of bullies and victims across all socioeconomic levels. Interestingly, Olweus attributes this finding to the relative homogeneity in the Scandinavian countries in which his studies were conducted. He speculates that in other countries, such as the United States, stronger associations between bullying and socioeconomic indicators, such as income, would be found. However, no pattern was detected between student reports of bullying and student household income in the 2001 SCS, a nationally representative U.S. data set (appendix B, table 1).

Likewise, no measurable differences were detected in the total percentage of students who reported bullying by students' residential urbanicity (appendix B, table 1). Nansel and her colleagues (2001) found no measurable differences among rural, suburban, and urban students' reports of bullying in their investigation as well.

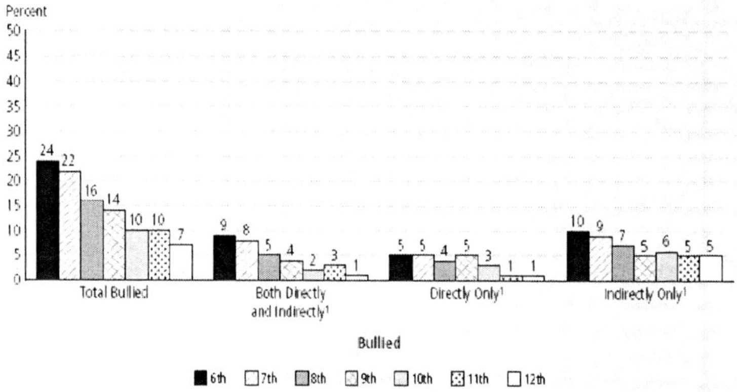

Figure 2. Percentage of students ages 12–18 who reported being bullied directly and/or indirectly at school during the previous 6 months, by grade level: 2001

Note: "At school" was defined as in the school building, on school property, on a school bus, or going to and from school. Youth ages 12 through 18 were first asked if "they had been bullied at school. That is, had anyone picked on them a lot or tried to make them do things they did not want to do (e.g., give them money)?" This is referred to as direct bullying. They were also asked, "Have you felt rejected because other students have made fun of you, called you names, or excluded you from activities?" This is referred to as indirect bullying. Total bullied includes youth who reported they were bullied directly or indirectly. Population size for students ages 12–18 is 24,315,000.

[1] Categories are mutually exclusive. Directly Only, Indirectly Only and Both Directly and Indirectly are distinct categories. Students appearing in one category do not appear in other categories.

Source: U.S. Department of Justice, Bureau of Justice Statistics, School Crime Supplement (SCS) to the National Crime Victimization Survey, 2001.

STUDENT REPORTS OF SCHOOL CHARACTERISTICS WHERE BULLYING OCCURS[7]

About 14 percent of students in both public schools and private schools reported being bullied (appendix B, table 2). Three percent of public and private school students reported direct bullying only, and 7 percent of public and private school students reported indirect bullying only.

[7] These data on school characteristics do not represent a sample of schools, rather they represent a sample of students. Thus, school characteristics are discussed in terms of student reports of school characteristics in this section.

In 2001, students who reported the presence of street gangs at school were more likely to report being bullied in any way (21 percent) than those who reported that street gangs were not present (13 percent) (appendix B, table 2). Similarly, those who reported street gangs at school were more likely to report direct bullying only (5 percent), indirect bullying only (8 percent), and both direct and indirect bullying (8 percent) than those students who did not report a street gang presence (3 percent, 6 percent, and 4 percent, respectively).

Schools take various measures to guard against criminal victimization and disciplinary problems. Increasing supervision of students is one avenue toward decreasing bullying in schools (Olweus 1993). Supervision, such as the employment of security personnel and the use of hallway monitors may deter bullies from attacking or threatening other students, calling them names, or making fun of them. In 2001, fewer students reported being bullied in schools with a security guard or an assigned police officer (13 percent), compared to students in schools with no such supervision (16 percent) (figure 3 and table 2). No measurable differences were detected (between schools with and without security officers) for either direct bullying or indirect bullying considered separately. More students were victims of both types of bullying in schools with security personnel (6 percent) than in schools without security guards or assigned police officers (4 percent).

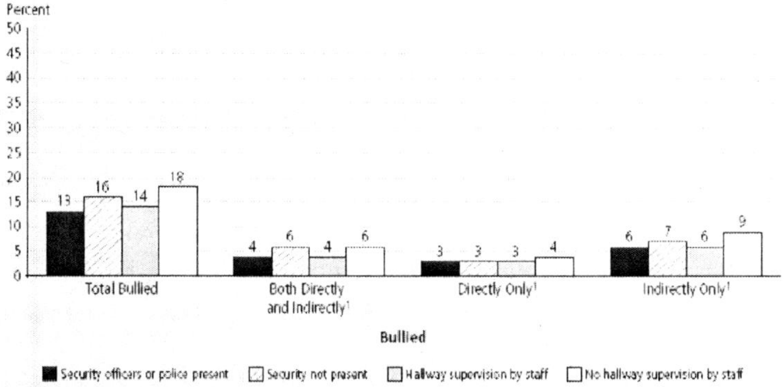

Figure 3. Percentage of students ages 12–18 who reported being bullied directly and/or indirectly at school during the previous 6 months, by security presence and hallway supervision: 2001

[1]Categories are mutually exclusive. Directly Only, Indirectly Only and Both Directly and Indirectly are distinct categories. Students appearing in one category do not appear in other categories.

Note: "At school" was defined as in the school building, on school property, on a school bus, or going to and from school. Youth ages 12 through 18 were first asked if "they had been bullied at school. That is, had anyone picked on them a lot or tried to make them do things they did not want to do (e.g., give them money)?" This is referred to as direct bullying. They were also asked, "Have you felt rejected because other students have made fun of you, called you names, or excluded you from activities?" This is referred to as indirect bullying. Total bullied includes youth who reported they were bullied directly or indirectly. Population size for students ages 12–18 is 24,315,000.

Source: U.S. Department of Justice, Bureau of Justice Statistics, School Crime Supplement (SCS) to the National Crime Victimization Survey, 2001.

Another common practice of supervision is hallway monitoring by school staff. Hall monitoring by school staff was associated with fewer bullied students (14 percent of students were bullied in schools with staff hallway monitors, vs. 18 percent of students being bullied in schools without such monitors). However, no measurable differences were detected in students' reports of direct bullying in schools with and without hallway supervision (figure 3 and appendix B, table 2). Students were less likely to report being indirectly bullied only in schools with hallway supervision (6 percent) than in schools without such supervision (9 percent). No measurable differences were detected in both direct and indirect bullying in schools with and without hallway supervision. Readers should note that while school characteristics such as school control, gang presence, security guards, and hallway monitors may be related to one another, the analysis does not control for such relationships. These data cannot address the question of whether having security guards or hallway monitors had an impact on bullying. Therefore, no causal inferences should be made when reading these results.

Bullying and Victimization

Elliott (1994) suggests that bullied students are at higher risk for criminal victimization at school, especially violent victimization. The purpose of this section is to examine student reports of bullying and their reports of serious violent, violent, and property victimization. Prior to presenting the results, some explanation of the differences between these two constructs, bullying and criminal victimization, and how they are collected is necessary.

Information on criminal victimization is collected in the main NCVS, to which the SCS is a supplement. Victimization is collected using a classification scheme in which the respondent identifies the characteristics of an event and those characteristics are used to classify the event as criminal. (For more information on the construction of the NCVS victimization variables used in this report, see the Glossary in appendix A). Readers may suspect that students who report direct bullying, or more overt physical attacks, may be reporting many of the same instances in their reports of criminal victimization. However, these two concepts are addressed quite differently during data collection for the SCS and therefore are reported as distinct events in this report.

As stated, the larger NCVS uses sets of characteristics to classify events as criminal. This was the approach taken for determining the serious violent, violent, and property victimizations reported here. In contrast, the SCS relies on the respondent to self-determine if they are bullied. Specifically, respondents are asked if they are bullied and allowed to determine if they fall into the bullying category based on the definition provided, rather than asked about characteristics of the situation and allowing the analyst to determine if the respondent has been bullied. This allows for the victim to use his or her own interpretation to define a situation, when the same situation may not have been labeled bullying by a bystander or the offender.

Results show, in 2001, 6 percent of all students ages 12 through 18 reported any form of criminal victimization at school (appendix B, table 3).[8] Serious violent victimization at school (including rape, sexual assault, robbery, and aggravated assault), was reported by less than 1 percent of students, and violent victimization at school (which includes those offenses in the serious violent category plus simple assaults) was reported by 2 percent of all students. Property victimization, which includes theft of a student's property at school, was reported by 4 percent of students (figure 4 and appendix B, table 3).

Students who report being bullied at school were at least twice as likely to report being the victims of crime at school compared to nonbullied students. When focusing on the total sample of students who reported being bullied at school (14 percent of the entire sample) (see appendix B, table 1), these students were more likely to experience any victimization, a serious violent victimization, a violent victimization, or a property victimization at school when compared to those students who were not bullied (figure 4 and appendix B, table 3). Specifically, 13 percent of bullied students reported any victimization at school compared to 4 percent of nonbullied students. About 2 percent of bullied students reported a serious violent victimization, 7 percent reported a violent victimization, and 8 percent reported a -property theft; 0.3 percent of nonbullied students reported a serious violent victimization, 1 percent reported a violent victimization, and 4 percent reported a property theft.

When looking at those students who were directly and/or indirectly bullied, interesting results emerge. First, the findings show that 18 percent of directly, or physically bullied students reported any victimization, and 7 percent of indirectly bullied students reported any victimization (figure 4 and appendix B, table 3). About 17 percent of students who reported both direct and indirect bullying reported any victimization. Second, the findings show that students who reported both types of bullying were more likely than students who reported only direct or indirect bullying to report being seriously violently victimized. About 1 percent of only directly bullied students and 0.3 percent of only indirectly bullied students reported a serious violent victimization, compared to larger percentage (4 percent) of students reporting both types of bullying. Third, directly bullied students were more likely than indirectly bullied students to be violently victimized (11 percent vs. 3 percent). Eleven percent of students reporting both forms of bullying also reported a violent victimization, a finding that is consistent with previous literature (Elliott 1994). Finally, victims of direct bullying only (9 percent) or both forms of bullying (10 percent) were more likely than those who reported only indirect bullying (5 percent) to be the victims of property victimization.

[8] Any victimization includes those students who reported being the victim of a violent crime or a property crime. Students who reported being the victim of both a property and a violent crime are counted once in the "any" category.

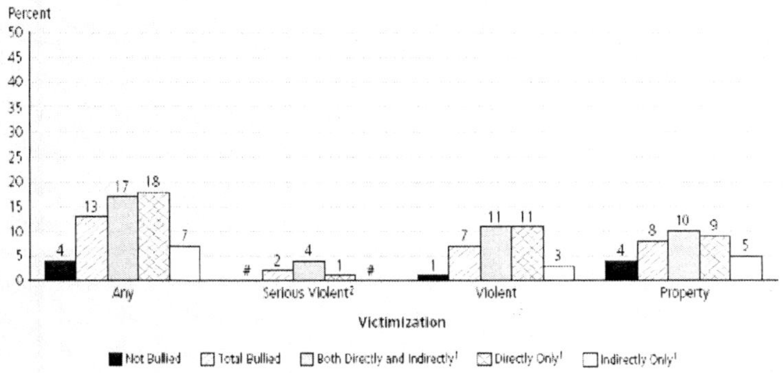

Figure 4. Percentage of students ages 12–18 who reported being victimized at school during the previous 6 months, by reports of being bullied directly only, bullied indirectly only, or being bullied directly or indirectly at school: 2001

[1] Categories are mutually exclusive.

[2] Serious violent crimes are also included in violent crimes.

[#] Rounds to zero.

Note: Serious violent crimes include rape, sexual assault, robbery, and aggravated assault. Violent crimes include serious violent crimes and simple assault.Any crimes include violent crimes and theft. "At school" includes inside the school building, on school property, or on the way to or from school. Youth ages 12 through 18 were first asked if "they had been bullied at school. That is, had anyone picked on them a lot or tried to make them do things they did not want to do (e.g., give them money)?" This is referred to as direct bullying. They were also asked, "Have you felt rejected because other students have made fun of you, called you names, or excluded you from activities?" This is referred to as indirect bullying. Total bullied includes youth who reported they were bullied directly or indirectly. Population size for students ages 12–18 is 24,315,000.

Source: U.S. Department of Justice, Bureau of Justice Statistics, School Crime Supplement (SCS) to the National Crime Victimization Survey, 2001.

BULLYING AND VICTIM OUTCOMES/BEHAVIORS

Psychological research suggests that passive victims of bullying are anxious and insecure (Olweus 1999; Wilton, Craig, and Pepler 2000; and Dodge et al. 1990). Passive victims often react to provocation by crying, withdrawing, or becoming quiet. This signals that they will not react or retaliate if they are attacked or insulted. Another type of victim, the "provocative" victim, is characterized by both anxious and aggressive reaction patterns (Olweus 1999). Provocative victims are likely to counter attack and have difficulty relating emotionally, whereas passive victims often avoid and acquiesce to their attackers (Wilton, Craig, and Pepler 2000). In fact, some research has shown that socially "rejected" boys are more likely to follow an act of aggression with another act of aggression than are boys who did not experience social rejection (Dodge et al. 1990). The purpose of this section is to investigate whether students who report only direct bullying respond with different defensive mechanisms or reactive behaviors than students who are bullied only indirectly or those who are bullied in both ways. While the SCS is a cross-sectional survey that does not allow the reader to know which event occurred first, the data do show that students who are victims of different types of bullying at school more often experience or engage in a variety of behaviors different from those of students not bullied. These behaviors include fear of attack; avoidance behaviors such as truancy from school; skipping classes, or not participating in extra-curricular activities; weapon carrying; involvement in physical fights; and varied academic performance. These data cannot address the question of whether bullying has an impact on these behaviors and outcomes, whether these behaviors elicit bullying from others, or whether some other combination of factors influences both bullying and these other behaviors

Fear is one by-product of threats and violence, and those students who are bullied at school may be afraid to attend school (Ericson 2001; Berthhold and Hoover 2000). The 2001 SCS findings are consistent with this research. Bullied students were more likely than nonbullied students to report being "sometimes or most of the time" afraid of an attack at school (18 percent vs. 3 percent), on the way to and from school (11 percent vs. 2 percent), and away from school (12 percent vs. 3 percent) (appendix B, table 4). Bullied students who were targeted both directly and indirectly were the most likely group of bullied students to sometimes or most of the time be afraid of an attack at school compared students who were bullied only directly and only indirectly (31 percent, 14 percent and 11 percent, respectively). Similar results were found for fear on the way to and from school, with 17 percent of students who were bullied both directly and indirectly reporting fear sometimes or most of the time, compared to 10 percent of students who were bullied only directly and 7 percent who were bullied only indirectly.

As discussed above, bullying can coincide with fear. Student reaction to this fear may lead to avoidance behavior or truancy. Specifically, students may act upon their feelings of fear and actually start avoiding places in school or be truant from school, classes, or extracurricular activities. Bullied students were more likely than nonbullied students to report avoidance behavior, such as avoiding the shortest route to school (6 percent of bullied students vs. 2 percent of nonbullied students), the entrance to the school (4 percent vs. 1 percent), hallways or stairs (7 percent vs. 1 percent), and the school cafeteria (6 percent vs. 1 percent) (appendix B, table 5). They were also more likely than nonbullied students to avoid restrooms (7 percent vs. 2 percent), the parking lot (5 percent vs. 1 percent), and other places inside the school building (5 percent vs. 1 percent) or on school grounds (6 percent vs. 1 percent). The SCS data also show that victims of both forms of bullying were more likely than victims of only direct and indirect bullying to avoid the shortest route to school (9 percent vs. 3 and 5 percent, respectively), the entrance to the school (7 percent vs. 3 and 2 percent), the school cafeteria (10 percent vs. 5 and 3 percent), and school restrooms (10 percent vs. 6 and 5 percent).

Taken to an extreme, this avoidance behavior may lead to truancy. Students who are bullied are at higher risk for truancy and subsequent dropout (Carney and Merrell 2001). In the 2001 SCS, bullied students were more likely than nonbullied students to skip school entirely because they thought someone might attack or harm them (4 percent vs. 1 percent) (figure 5 and appendix B, table 5). Bullied students were more likely to skip classes than were nonbullied students (3 percent vs. 0.2 percent). Bullied students were also more likely to skip extracurricular activities compared to nonbullied students (4 percent vs. 1 percent). Truancy was more likely to occur among students who were victims of direct bullying than among victims of indirect bullying. Specifically, 4 percent of students who were directly bullied skipped school compared to 1 percent of students who were indirectly bullied. Students who were victims of both types of bullying were more likely to skip school (7 percent), class (7 percent), and extracurricular activities (6 percent) than were students who were only indirectly bullied (1 percent, 1 percent, and 2 percent, respectively), and were also more likely than students who were only directly bullied to skip class (3 percent).

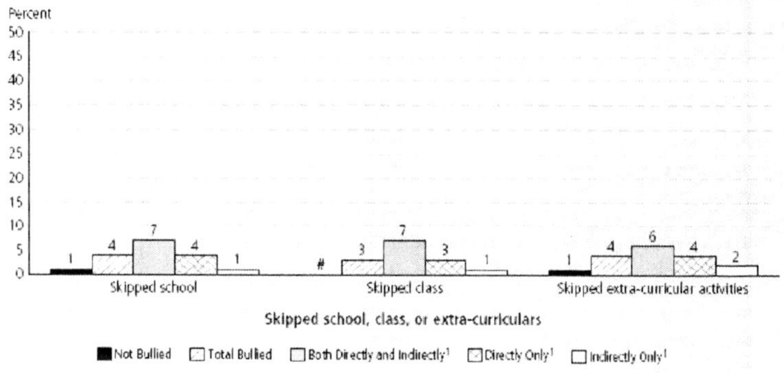

Figure 5. Percentage of students ages 12–18 who reported skipping school, class, or extra-curricular activities during the previous 6 months, by reports of being bullied directly only, bullied indirectly only, or being bullied directly and indirectly at school: 2001

[1] Categories are mutually exclusive.

Rounds to zero.

Note: "At school" was defined as in the school building, on school property, on a school bus, or going to and from school. Youth ages 12 through 18 were first asked if "they had been bullied at school. That is, had anyone picked on them a lot or tried to make them do things they did not want to do (e.g., give them money)?" This is referred to as direct bullying. They were also asked, "Have you felt rejected because other students have made fun of you, called you names, or excluded you from activities?" This is referred to as indirect bullying. Total bullied includes youth who reported they were bullied directly or indirectly. Population size for students ages 12–18 is 24,315,000.

Source: U.S. Department of Justice, Bureau of Justice Statistics, School Crime Supplement (SCS) to the National Crime Victimization Survey, 2001.

Research suggests that being victimized by bullying may be an antecedent to aggressive behavior (Nansel et al. 2003, Loeber and Stouthamer-Loeber 1998). As discussed above, bullied students may resort to aggression in retaliation or be more inclined to respond to negative behaviors with antisocial responses. In the 2001 SCS, about 2 percent of all students ages 12 through 18 reported carrying a weapon (gun, knife, or some other weapon) to school for protection, and 5 percent reported being involved in a physical fight (figure 7 and appendix B, table 6). While the 2001 SCS cannot be used to establish causality, results show that more bullied students carried a weapon to school for protection (4 percent) in the 6 months prior to the survey than did nonbullied students (1 percent). Consistent with this finding, Carney and Merrell (2001) also report that victims of bullying are more likely than their nonbullied counterparts to bring weapons to school in order to protect themselves. No measurable differences were detected in the 2001 SCS in student reports of weapon carrying among victims of only direct, only indirect, and both forms of bullying.

Bullied students were also more likely to be involved in physical fights at school. About 15 percent of bullied students reported being involved in a physical fight, compared to 4 percent of nonbullied students (figure 6 and appendix B, table 6). Bullied students were more likely than nonbullied students (4 percent) to engage in fights regardless of whether they were bullied only directly (15 percent) or only indirectly (10 percent). Victims of indirect bullying only were less likely to engage in fights than were victims of both forms of bullying (10 percent vs. 21 percent). Lawrence (1998) suggests that victims of bullying may become aggressive toward other students. In this case, regardless of the type of bullying—whether physical or social—bullied students may tend to react through physical confrontation.

Academic achievement is a focal concern for educators and schools across the nation. Past research demonstrates that students who are targeted by bullies often have difficulty concentrating on their schoolwork, resulting in academic achievement that is marginal to poor (Batsche and Knoff 1994). Farrington (1993) also suggests that the psychological consequences of bullying can include lack of concentration on schoolwork. The SCS 2001 allows for the examination of bullying behavior and self-reports of academic grades. A few patterns emerged in the data, first, bullied students were less likely to report getting mostly A's than students who did not report or experience bullying at school (27 percent of bullied students vs. 34 percent of non bullied students) (appendix B, table 7). However, bullied students were more likely to report receiving A's and B's than D's and F's (27 percent and 41 percent vs. 8 percent, respectively). Second, of those students who reported lower grades, bullied students were more likely to report receiving mostly D's and F's than their non-bullied counterparts (8 percent vs. 3 percent). Victims of both forms of bullying were more likely to report getting D's and F's than those who were bullied directly or indirectly (12 percent, 7 percent, and 6 percent, respectively).

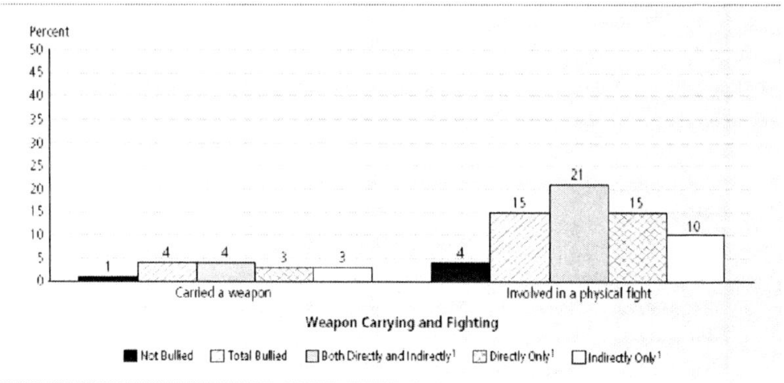

Figure 6. Percentage of students ages 12–18 who reported carrying a weapon for protection or being involved in a physical fight at school during the previous 6 months, by reports of being bullied directly only, indirectly only, or being bullied directly and indirectly at school: 2001

[1] Categories are mutually exclusive.

Note: "At school" was defined as in the school building, on school property, on a school bus, or going to and from school. Youth ages 12 through 18 were first asked if "they had been bullied at school. That is, had anyone picked on them a lot or tried to make them do things they did not want to do (e.g., give them money)?" This is referred to as direct bullying. They were also asked, "Have you felt rejected because other students have made fun of you, called you names, or excluded you from activities?" This is referred to as indirect bullying. Total bullied includes youth who reported they were bullied directly or indirectly. Students included as carrying weapons reported carrying a gun, knife or other weapon to school in the 6 months prior to the survey. Population size for students ages 12–18 is 24,315,000.

Source: U.S. Department of Justice, Bureau of Justice Statistics, School Crime Supplement (SCS) to the National Crime Victimization Survey, 2001.

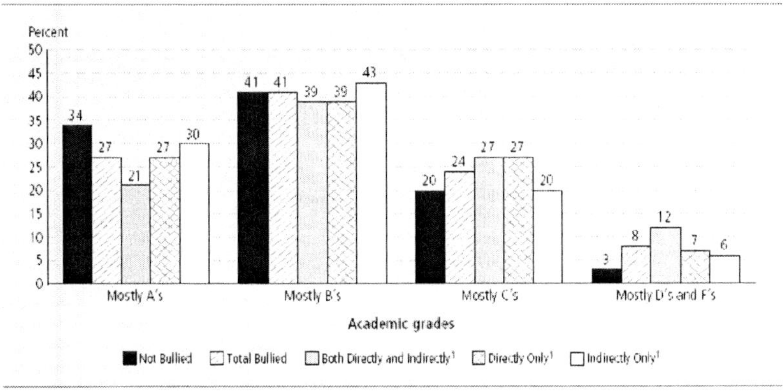

Figure 7. Percentage of students ages 12–18 who reported receiving different academic grades during the school year, by reports of being bullied directly only, indirectly only, or being bullied directly and indirectly at school: 2001

[1] Categories are mutually exclusive.

Note: "At school" was defined as in the school building, on school property, on a school bus, or going to and from school. Youth ages 12 through 18 were first asked if "they had been bullied at school. That is, had anyone picked on them a lot or tried to make them do things they did not want to do (e.g., give them money)?" This is referred to as direct bullying. They were also asked, "Have you felt rejected because other students have made fun of you, called you names, or excluded you from activities?" This is referred to as indirect bullying. Total bullied includes youth who reported they were bullied directly or indirectly. Population size for students ages 12–18 is 24,315,000.

Source: U.S. Department of Justice, Bureau of Justice Statistics, School Crime Supplement (SCS) to the National Crime Victimization Survey, 2001.

Summary and Conclusions

The analyses in this study employ specific subtypes of bullying which may be useful when looking at bullying interactions. This study shows that 14 percent of students ages 12 through 18 reported they had been bullied at school in the previous 6 months. Three percent reported being the victims of direct or physical bullying only, 7 percent reported being the victims of indirect, or social bullying, and 5 percent reported being the victims of both types of bullying. This study also shows that the specific subtypes of bullying are often related to different individual-level and school-level characteristics.

Bullied students are generally younger students of either sex, and are more often White than Black. No measurable differences were detected when comparing the prevalence of bullying by students' household income or urbanicity. Bullied students report that their schools are more likely to have gangs and less likely to have supervision in the form of police officers, security guards, or school staff in the hallways. Finally, student reports of attending public or private schools are not associated with student reports of bullying.

The findings also suggest that students who are victims of bullying at school more often are victimized in other ways. When compared to nonbullied students, bullied students are more likely to fear attack at school, on the way to and from school, and away from school. Bullied students engage in a variety of avoidance behaviors and are more likely to be truant from school, classes, or extracurricular activities than their nonbullied peers. A highlight of this study is the finding that victims of bullying are more likely to exhibit negative outcome behaviors, such as weapon carrying or being involved in physical fights, compared to students who are not bullied. In fact, more students who were bullied reported carrying a weapon to school for protection (4 percent), compared to nonbullied students (1 percent). In addition, more bullied students were involved in a physical fight than were nonbullied students (15 percent vs. 4 percent). One prior research investigation suggests that victims of bullying are more likely to engage in violent behaviors (Nansel et al. 2003), and those findings are confirmed in this national analysis.

Of final import to educators, parents, and practitioners, the findings show that bullied students were less likely to report receiving A's than nonbullied students, but were more likely to report receiving A's and B's than D's and F's. When focusing on poorly performing students, bullied students were more likely to report getting mostly D's or F's than their nonbullied counterparts.

Appendix A: Technical Notes

Survey

The National Crime Victimization Survey (NCVS) and the School Crime Supplement (SCS) to the NCVS were used to provide estimates in this report. The NCVS, administered for the U.S. Bureau of Justice Statistics by the Census Bureau, is the nation's primary source of information on crime victimization and the victims of crime. Initiated in 1972 and redesigned in 1992, the NCVS collects detailed information on the frequency and nature of the crimes of rape, sexual assault, robbery, aggravated and simple assault, theft, household burglary, and motor vehicle theft experienced by Americans and their households each year. The survey measures crimes reported as well as those not reported to police.

The 2001 NCVS sample consists of about 53,730 households selected using a stratified, multistage cluster design. In the first stage, the primary sampling units (PSUs), consisting of counties or groups of counties, were selected. In the second stage, smaller areas, called Enumeration Districts (EDs), were selected from each sampled PSU. Finally, from selected EDs, clusters of four households, called segments, were selected for interview. At each stage, the selection was done proportionate to population size in order to create a self-weighting sample. The final sample was augmented to account for housing units constructed after the 1990 Decennial Census. Within each sampled household, Census Bureau personnel interviewed all household members ages 12 and older to determine whether they had been victimized according to the measured crimes during the 6 months preceding the interview. About 79,360 persons ages 12 and older are interviewed each 6 months. Households remain in the sample for 3 years and are interviewed 7 times at 6-month intervals.

Created as a supplement to the NCVS and codesigned by the National Center for Education Statistics (NCES) and Bureau of Justice Statistics (BJS), the SCS survey was conducted in 1989, 1995, 1999, 2001, and 2003 to collect additional information about school-related victimizations on a national level. The survey was designed to assist policymakers as well as academic researchers and practitioners at the federal, state, and local levels in making informed decisions concerning crime in schools. The SCS asks students a number of key questions about their experiences with and perceptions of crime and violence that occurred inside their school, on school grounds, on a school bus, or on the way to or from school. Additional questions not included in the NCVS were also added to the SCS, such as the presence of weapons and street gangs in school, whether students were bullied or rejected at school, attitudinal questions relating to fear of victimization and avoidance behavior at school, preventive measures used by the school, participation in afterschool activities, perceptions of school rules, the presence of hate-related words and graffiti in school, as well as the availability of drugs and alcohol in school.

In all SCS survey years, the SCS was conducted for a 6-month period from January through June in all households selected for the NCVS. Within these households, the eligible respondents for the SCS were those household members ages 12 through 18 who had attended school at any time during the

6 months preceding the interview, and were enrolled in grades 6 through 12 in a school that would help them advance toward a high school diploma. Eligible respondents were asked the supplemental questions in the SCS only after completing their entire NCVS interview.

In 2001, the definition for "at school" pertaining to victimizations included those that occurred on school property, going to and from school, or while attending school. The NCVS variables appended to the SCS data file asking where the incident happened and what the victim was doing when it happened were used to ascertain whether the incident happened at school.

The NCVS "type of crime" variable appended to the SCS data file was used to classify victimizations of students in the SCS as violent or property victimization. Any victimization is a combination of violent victimization and property. If the student reported an incident of either violent or property victimization or both, he or she is counted in the any victimization measure. Violent crimes include serious violent crimes—rape, sexual assault, and aggravated assault —and simple assault. See the Glossary for more detailed information about the construction of these and other variables.

Readers should note that several limitations inherent to victimization surveys, such as the NCVS SCS, might impact estimates of bullying (Cantor and Lynch 2000). First, the SCS includes unbounded interviews, or interviews that include victimizations that exceed the 6-month reference period asked of SCS respondents. This may artificially increase reports of victimization since respondents may recall events outside of the given reference period. For example, a respondent may mistakenly report an event that happened 1 year ago and not within the requested past 6 months. Second, the SCS does not use a classification scheme for determining bullying events. That is, the larger NCVS uses sets of characteristics to classify events as criminal whereas the SCS often relies on the respondent to self-determine a condition. For example, respondents are asked if they are bullied and allowed to determine if they fall into the bullying category based on the definition provided, rather than asked about characteristics of the situation and allowing the analyst to determine if the respondent has been bullied. This allows for the victim to use his own interpretation or conceptions to define a situation, when the same situation may not have been labeled bullying by a bystander or the offender. Third, victim surveys emphasize crime events as incidents at one point in time. Reality tells us that victims can often live in a state of victimization where they are threatened or victimized regularly. While the NCVS does allow for these series to be flagged for criminal victimizations, reports of bullying behaviors are not collected in this way. Finally, respondent recall of bullying events may be inaccurate. People may forget the event entirely or recall the characteristics of the event inaccurately. This would lead to an underestimation of victimization.

Unit and Item Response Rates

Unit response rates indicate how many sampled units have completed interviews. Because interviews with students could only be completed after households had responded to the NCVS, the unit completion rate for the SCS reflects both the household interview completion rate and the student interview completion rate. A total of 8,374 students participated in the SCS 2001. The household completion rate was 93 percent, and the student completion rate was 77 percent. Thus, the overall SCS response rate (calculated by multiplying the household completion rate by the student completion rate) was 72 percent in 2001.

The rate at which the respondents provide a valid response to a given item is referred to as its item response rate. Item response rates for items used in this report were generally high. Most items were answered by over 95 percent of all eligible respondents. The only exception was the household income question, which was answered by approximately 84 percent of all households in 2001 and approximately 86 percent of all households in the 1999 administration of the survey. Income and income-related questions typically have relatively low response rates compared to other items due to their sensitive nature. No explicit imputation procedure was used to correct for item nonresponse. However, restricting the analysis to those responses that were provided and ignoring the missing responses is an implicit form of imputation. The assumption is that the missing responses are completely random, and represent a subsample of the full sample.

Weights were developed to compensate for differential probabilities of selection and nonresponse. The weighted data permit inferences about the 12- to 18-year-old student population enrolled in schools in 2001. The weight used with the 2001 SCS datafile is V297 (SCS person weight).

Survey Standard Errors

As a result of the complex sampling design of the SCS and the NCVS, the resulting statistics are more variable than they would have been had they been based on data from a simple random sample of the same size. Several procedures and statistical software packages are available for calculating precise estimates of sampling errors for complex samples. The analyses carried out in this report used the Taylor Series procedure to calculate standard errors and was done through the AM statistical software package that is available for free downloading at http://am.air.org.

The sample of students selected for each SCS is just one of many possible samples that could have been selected. It is possible that estimates from a given SCS student sample may differ from estimates that would have been produced from other student samples. This type of variability is called sampling error, or the standard error, because it arises from using a sample of students rather than all students.

The standard error is a measure of the variability of a parameter estimate. It indicates how much variation there is in the population of possible estimates of a parameter for a given sample size. The probability that a complete census count would differ from the sample estimate by less than 1 standard error is about 68 percent. The chance that the difference would be less than 1.65 standard errors is about 90 percent, and that the difference would be less than 1.96 standard errors, about 95 percent. Standard errors for the percentage estimates are presented in the appendix tables.

Standard errors are typically developed assuming that the sample is drawn purely at random. The sample for the SCS was not a simple random sample, however. Calculation of the standard errors requires procedures that are markedly different from the ones used when the data are from a simple random sample. To estimate the statistics and standard errors, this report used the Taylor series

Statistical Tests

Comparisons that have been drawn in the text of this report have been tested for statistical significance to ensure that the differences are larger than those that might be expected due to sampling variation. The statistical comparisons in this report were based on the *t* statistic. Whether the statistical test is considered significant or not is determined by calculating a *t* value for the difference between a pair of means or proportions and comparing this value to published tables of values, called critical values (cv). The alpha level is an *a priori* statement of the probability that a difference exists in fact rather than by chance.

The *t* statistic between estimates from various subgroups presented in the tables can be computed by using the following formula:

$$t = \frac{x_1 - x_2}{\sqrt{SE_1^2 + SE_2^2}}$$

where *x1* and *x2* are the estimates to be compared (e.g., the means of sample members in two groups) and *SE1* and *SE2* are their corresponding standard errors.

While many descriptive comparisons in this report were tested using a t statistic, some comparisons among categories of an ordered variable with three or more levels involved a test for a linear trend across all categories, rather than a series of tests between pairs of categories. In this report, when differences among percentages were examined relative to a variable with ordered categories, Analysis of Variance (ANOVA) was used to test for a linear relationship between the two variables. To do this, ANOVA models included orthogonal linear contrasts corresponding to successive levels of the independent variable. These were used to create mean squares for the within- and between-group variance components and their corresponding *F* statistics, which were then compared with published values of *F* for a significance level of 0.05. Significant values of both the overall *F* and the *F* associated with the linear contrast term were required as evidence of a linear relationship between the two variables.

Glossary—Definitions of Variables Used

Each row (student and school characteristics) and column variable used in the analyses for this report is described below. All variables are constructed from the 2001 SCS data file. The data file contains all variables collected by the SCS as well as select variables collected in the 2001 NCVS-1 Basic Screen Questionnaire and the NCVS-2 Crime Incident Report that have been appended to the SCS. The data are available for download from the Inter-University Consortium for Political and Social Research via NCES' Crime and Safety Surveys portal web site located at: http://nces.ed.gov/programs/crime/surveys.asp.

Prior to analysis, the 2001 SCS data file was filtered to include only students who were ages 12 through 18 (using v212 [RESPONDENT AGE]), were enrolled in primary or secondary education programs (using v217

[GRADE LEVEL IN SCHOOL]), were enrolled in school in the past 6 months (using v215 [DID YOU ATTEND SCHOOL DURING THE LAST 6 MONTHS?]), and were not home-schooled during that time (using v3958 [HOME SCHOOLED DURING LAST 6 MONTHS?]). Students who did not fulfill these characteristics were deleted from the analysis. The final unweighted sample size was 8,374.

Student Characteristics

SEX (v140): This variable was taken directly from v140 for the sex of the respondent: Male or Female. This variable was collected in the NCVS-1 Basic Screen Questionnaire and appended to the SCS data file.

RACE/ETHNICITY (v145 and v146): This variable was taken directly from v145 for the race of the respondent and v146 for the Hispanic origin of the respondent. If the respondent identified themselves as Hispanic in v146, they were categorized as Hispanic, regardless of their response to v145. Non-Hispanics in v145 were classified as White, Black, or Other. Those individuals included in the "Other" category identified themselves as Asians, Pacific Islanders, and American Indians (including Alaska Native). The resulting categories were: 1) White, non-Hispanic; 2) Black, non-Hispanic; 4) Hispanic; and 5) Other. Race categories exclude Hispanic origin unless specified. Variables v145 and v156 were collected in the NCVS-1 Basic Screen Questionnaire and appended to the SCS data file.

GRADE (v217): This variable was taken directly from v217. Response options included "Fifth and under", "Sixth" through "Twelfth" grades, "Other", and "College/GED/Post-graduate/Other non-eligible" All respondents not in grades six through twelve were excluded from the analysis. This variable was collected in item 2a of the SCS instrument (located in appendix D).

HOUSEHOLD INCOME (v22): This variable was taken directly from v22 for the household income of the respondent and collapsed into the following categories: 1) Less than $7,500; 2) $7,500–14,999; 3) $15,000–24,999; 4) $25,000–34,999; 5) $35,000–49,999; 6) $50,000–74,999; and 7) $75,000 or more. This variable was collected in the NCVS-1 Basic Screen Questionnaire and appended to the SCS data file.

PLACE OF RESIDENCE (v119): This variable was taken directly from v119 for the Metropolitan Statistical Area (MSA) Status of the respondent's household as defined by the 1990 U.S. Bureau of the Census. Categories include: Central city of an (S)MSA (Urban) ; In (S)MSA but not in central city (Suburban); and Not (S)MSA (Rural). This variable was appended to the SCS data file by the U.S. Bureau of the Census.

BULLIED (v272 and v3971): This variable was constructed using v272 and v3971. If respondents' answered affirmatively to either v272 and v3971 they were categorized as "Bullied." v272 asks, "During the last 6 months, have you been bullied at school? That is, has anyone picked on you a lot or tried to make you do things you didn't want to do like give them money?" v3971 asks, "During the last 6 months, have you often felt rejected by other students at school? For example, have you ever felt rejected because other students have made fun of you, called you names, or excluded you from activities?" Variables v272 and v3971 were collected in items 19 and 20a of the SCS instrument.

BOTH DIRECTLY AND INDIRECTLY (v272 and v3971): This variable was constructed using v272 and v3971. If respondents' answered affirmatively to both v272 and v3971 they were categorized as "Bullied Both Directly and Indirectly." Variables v272 and v3971 were collected in items 19 and 20a of the SCS instrument.

DIRECTLY ONLY (v272): This variable was constructed using v272. If respondents' answered affirmatively to v272 they were categorized as "Bullied Directly." This variable was collected in item 19 of the SCS instrument.

INDIRECTLY ONLY (v3971): This variable was constructed using v3971. If respondents' answered affirmatively to v3971 they were categorized as "Bullied Indirectly." This variable was collected in item 20a of the SCS instrument.

School Characteristics

SCHOOL TYPE (v221): This variable was taken directly from v221 that asks the type of school for each student: Pubic or Private. This variable was collected in item 7a of the SCS instrument.

GANG PRESENCE (v263): This variable is taken directly from v263 that asks students whether there are street gangs present at their school. Instructions for defining street gangs were as follows: "You may know these as street gangs, fighting gangs, crews, or something else. Gangs may use common names, signs, symbols, or colors. For this survey, we are interested in all gangs, whether or not they are involved in violent or illegal activity." Response options included "Yes", "No", and "Don't Know." This variable was collected in item 30 of the SCS instrument.

PRESENCE OF SECURITY OFFICERS OR ASSIGNED POLICE (v233): This variable was taken directly from v233 that asked students whether there are security guards and/or assigned police officers present at their school to ensure the safety of students. Response options included "Yes", "No", and "Don't Know." This variable was collected in item 14a of the SCS instrument.

HALLWAY SUPERVISION BY SCHOOL STAFF (v234): This variable was taken directly from v234 that asked students whether there is hallway supervision by other school staff or other adults to ensure the safety of students. Response options included "Yes", "No", and "Don't Know." This variable was collected in item 14b the SCS instrument.

Column Variables

VICTIMIZATION (v819, v1341, v1863, v2385, v2907, v3429, and v3951): Each SCS respondent represents a student who may have reported at least one and as many as 7 incident(s) of victimization on the NCVS-1. For each incident of victimization reported, a Crime Incident Report NCVS-2 was completed. These (up to 7) Crime Incident Reports were appended to the SCS data file for each respondent who reported at least one incidence of victimization. The victimization categories used in this report for each of these incidents of victimization were determined using the Type of Crime (TOC) code reported in the Crime Incident Reports for each incident. The TOC codes used to determine the type of victimization were taken directly from variables v819 (first incident), v1341 (second incident), v1863 (third incident), v2385 (fourth incident), v2907 (fifth incident), v3429 (sixth incident), and v3951 (seventh incident). Each TOC variable contains several types of crime that have been categorized into "serious violent," "violent," "property," and "any" for the purposes of this report. "Serious violent crime" includes: completed and attempted rapes, all sexual attacks, all completed and attempted robberies, all aggravated assaults, all verbal threats and threats with weapons, sexual assault without injury and unwanted sexual contact without force. "Violent crime" includes: serious violent crimes listed above, simple assault with injury, assault without a weapon and without injury, and verbal threat of assault. "Property crime" includes: purse snatching, pick pocketing, all burglaries, attempted forcible entry, completed and attempted motor vehicle theft, and completed thefts valuing less than $10 or greater. "Any crime" includes one or more reports of any of the crimes listed above. Each of these measure the prevalence of victimization, that is, if a respondent reported one or more incidents in one of these types of victimizations, they were included as a victim only once under the specified category.

AFRAID OF ATTACK AT SCHOOL, ON THE WAY TO OR FROM SCHOOL AND AWAY FROM SCHOOL (v284, v285, and v286): These variables were taken directly from v284, v285 and v286 that asked students if they were afraid someone would attack or threaten to attack them at school, on the way to or from school, and away from school, respectively. Response options were collapsed into the following categories: "Never," "Almost Never," and "Sometimes/Most of the time." These variables were collected in items 24, 25, and 26 of the SCS instrument.

AVOIDING CERTAIN AREAS OF THE SCHOOL AND SKIPPING SCHOOL, CLASS OR EXTRA-CURRICULAR ACTIVITIES (v273, v274, v275, v276, v277, v278, v279, v280, v281, v282, and v283): Student reports of avoiding certain areas in school were taken directly from the following variables: v273 (avoided shortest route to school), v274 (avoided entrance to school), v275 (avoided hallways or stairs), v276 (avoided school cafeteria), v277 (avoided restrooms), v278 (avoided other places in school building), v279 (avoided parking lot), v280 (avoided other places on school grounds), v281 (avoided extra-curricular activities), v282 (avoided class), and v283 (stayed home from school). Response options included "Yes" or "No." These variables were collected in items 23a, 23b, 23c, and 23d of the SCS instrument.

CARRIED A WEAPON (v287, v288, and v289): This variable was constructed from three separate variables that asked the student if they had carried a gun (v287) or knife (v288) intended as a weapon or any other weapon (v289) to school or on to school grounds during the last 6 months. If a respondent answered "Yes" to any of these items, they were included in the derived variable. These variables were collected in items 27a, 27b, and 27c of the SCS instrument.

INVOLVED IN A PHYISICAL FIGHT (v3969): This variable was taken directly from v3969 that asked students whether they had been involved in one or more physical fights at school in the last 6 months. Response options included "Yes" and "No". This variable was collected in item 18a of the SCS instrument.

SELF-REPORTS OF GRADES (v3982): This variable was taken directly from v3982 that asked students what grades they mostly received across all subjects in the past school year. Response options included "A's," "B's," "C's," "D's," "F's," and "School does not give grades/no alphabetic grade equivalent." This variable was collected in item 34 of the SCS instrument.

For further information. NCES has collected and published data on school crime and safety through a number of publications. Readers who are interested in further information about these studies and downloading available data files, including the SCS data file used in this article, should contact Kathryn Chandler at kathryn.chandler@ed.gov or visit the Crime and Safety Surveys web site at http://nces.ed.gov/programs/crime/.

APPENDIX B: ESTIMATE TABLES

Table 1. Percentage of students ages 12–18 who reported being bullied directly and/or indirectly at school during the previous 6 months, by selected student characteristics: 2001

Student characteristics	Number of students	Total	Both Directly and Indirectly[1]	Directly Only[1]	Indirectly Only[1]
Total	24,315,000	14.4	4.5	3.4	6.5
Student sex					
Male	12,591,000	15.0	5.0	3.6	6.4
Female	11,724,000	13.7	3.9	3.1	6.7
Student race/ethnicity[2]					
White, non-Hispanic	15,784,000	15.4	4.9	3.5	6.9
Black, non-Hispanic	3,793,000	12.3	3.2	2.6	6.6
Hispanic	3,446,000	13.0	4.3	2.9	4.2
Other, non-Hispanic	1,063,000	10.8	3.7	3.3	5.3
Student grade					
Sixth	2,113,000	24.3	9.3	4.8	10.1
Seventh	3,848,000	21.6	8.0	5.0	8.6
Eighth	3,947,000	16.0	5.3	3.9	6.8
Ninth	4,093,000	13.9	3.9	4.6	5.3
Tenth	3,774,000	10.4	2.1	2.5	5.8
Eleventh	3,581,000	9.5	3.1	1.2	5.2
Twelfth	2,960,000	7.4	1.0	1.4	4.9
Student household income					
Less than $7,500	836,000	15.0	3.8	4.0	7.1
$7,500–14,999	993,000	13.3	4.9	3.1	5.4
$15,000–24,999	2,524,000	17.5	5.9	4.2	7.3
$25,000–34,999	2,874,000	15.0	5.4	4.1	5.5
$35,000–49,999	4,074,000	14.8	4.7	2.8	7.4
$50,000–74,999	4,279,000	13.2	4.2	2.5	6.5
$75,000 or more	4,861,000	12.9	3.5	2.6	6.8

Table 1 (cont.)

Student place of residence					
Urban	6,574,000	13.2	4.1	2.7	6.4
Suburban	12,812,000	14.9	4.5	3.6	6.8
Rural	4,929,000	14.7	5.0	3.7	6.0

[1] Categories are mutually exclusive. Directly Only, Indirectly Only, and Both Directly and Indirectly are distinct categories. Students appearing in one category do not appear in other categories.

[2] Other includes Asians, Pacific Islanders, and American Indians (including Alaska Natives). Race categories exclude Hispanic origin unless specified.

Note: "At school" was defined as in the school building, on school property, on a school bus, or going to and from school. Youth ages 12 through 18 were first asked if "they had been bullied at school. That is, had anyone picked on them a lot or tried to make them do things they did not want to do (e.g., give them money)?" This is referred to as direct bullying. They were also asked, "Have you felt rejected because other students have made fun of you, called you names, or excluded you from activities?" This is referred to as indirect bullying. Total bullied includes youth who reported they were bullied directly or indirectly. Population size for students ages 12–18 is 24,315,000. Detail may not sum to totals due to missing data.

Source: U.S. Department of Justice, Bureau of Justice Statistics, School Crime Supplement (SCS) to the National Crime Victimization Survey, 2001.

Table 2. Percentage of students ages 12–18 who reported being bullied directly and/or indirectly at school during the previous 6 months, by selected school characteristics: 2001

School characteristics	Number of students	Bullied			
		Total	Both directly and indirectly	Directly only[1]	Indirectly only[1]
Total	24,315,000	14.4	4.5	3.4	6.5
School type					
Public	22,176,000	14.4	4.6	3.4	6.5
Private	2,098,000	14.0	4.5	2.7	6.7
Gang presence					
Yes	4,896,000	21.1	8.1	4.9	8.1
No	15,993,000	13.0	3.7	3.1	6.2
Presence of security officers or assigned police					
Yes	15,475,000	13.3	3.8	3.4	6.1
No	8,840,000	16.2	5.7	3.4	7.1

Table 2 (cont.)

Hallway supervision by school staff					
Yes	21,479,000	13.9	4.4	3.3	6.2
No	2,836,000	17.9	5.6	3.7	8.5

[1] Categories are mutually exclusive.

Note: "At school" includes inside the school building, on school property, or on the way to or from school. Youth ages 12 through 18 were first asked if "they had been bullied at school. That is, had anyone picked on them a lot or tried to make them do things they did not want to do (e.g., give them money)?" This is referred to as direct bullying. They were also asked, "Have you felt rejected because other students have made fun of you, called you names, or excluded you from activities?" This is referred to as indirect bullying. Total bullied includes youth who reported they were bullied directly or indirectly. Population size for students ages 12–18 is 24,315,000. Detail may not sum to totals due to missing data.

Source: U.S. Department of Justice, Bureau of Justice Statistics, School Crime Supplement (SCS) to the National Crime Victimization Survey, 2001.

Table 3. Percentage of students ages 12–18 who reported being victimized at school during the previous 6 months, by reports of being bullied directly and/or indirectly at school: 2001

	Number of students	Victimization			
		Any	Serious Violent[1]	Violent	Property
Total	24,315,000	5.5	0.4	1.8	4.2
Not Bullied	20,680,000	4.2	0.3	0.8	3.6
Bullied	3,494,000	13.0	1.5	7.3	7.6
Both Directly and Indirectly[2]	1,095,000	17.4	3.7	10.9	9.9
Directly Only[2]	816,000	18.3	0.7	10.8	9.2
Indirectly Only[2]	1,583,000	7.3	0.3	2.9	5.3

[1] Serious violent crimes are also included in violent crimes. [2]Categories are mutually exclusive.

Note: Serious violent crimes include rape, sexual assault, robbery, and aggravated assault. Violent crimes include serious violent crimes and simple assault. Any crimes include violent crimes and theft. "At school" includes inside the school building, on school property, or on the way to or from school. Youth ages 12 through 18 were first asked if "they had been bullied at school. That is, had anyone picked on them a lot or tried to make them do things they did not want to do (e.g., give them money)?" This is referred to as direct bullying. They were also asked, "Have you felt rejected because other students have made fun of you, called you names, or excluded you from activities?" This is referred to as indirect bullying. Total bullied includes youth who reported they were bullied directly or indirectly. Population size for students ages 12–18 is 24,315,000. Detail may not sum to totals due to missing data.

Source: U.S. Department of Justice, Bureau of Justice Statistics, School Crime Supplement (SCS) to the National Crime Victimization Survey, 2001.

Table 4. Percentage of students ages 12–18 who reported fearing attack during the previous 6 months at school, on the way to and from school, and away from school, by reports of being bullied directly and/or indirectly at school: 2001

Victim behaviors	Number of students	Afraid of attack at school			Afraid of attack on the way to or from school			Afraid of attack away from school[1]		
		Never	Almost Never	Sometimes/ Most of the Time	Never	Almost Never	Sometimes/ Most of the Time	Never	Almost Never	Sometimes/ Most of the Time
Total	24,315,000	80.7	13.9	4.7	87.5	8.2	3.6	80.9	13.7	4.6
Not Bullied	20,680,000	85.2	11.9	2.5	90.1	7.2	2.4	83.9	12.3	3.4
Bullied	3,494,000	55.9	26.1	17.9	74.4	14.7	10.7	65.3	22.3	12.2
Both Directly										
and Indirectly[1]	1,095,000	42.0	26.4	31.2	64.1	18.3	16.9	60.1	23.8	15.5
Directly Only[1]	816,000	52.5	33.4	14.1	76.0	13.7	10.3	62.8	26.8	10.4
Indirectly Only[1]	1,583,000	67.3	22.0	10.6	80.6	12.7	6.6	70.2	18.9	11.0

[1] Categories are mutually exclusive.

Note: "At school" was defined as in the school building, on school property, on a school bus, or going to and from school. Youth ages 12 through 18 were first asked if "they had been bullied at school. That is, had anyone picked on them a lot or tried to make them do things they did not want to do (e.g., give them money)?" This is referred to as direct bullying. They were also asked, "Have you felt rejected because other students have made fun of you, called you names, or excluded you from activities?" This is referred to as indirect bullying. Total bullied includes youth who reported they were bullied directly or indirectly. Population size for students ages 12–18 is 24,315,000. Detail may not sum to totals due to missing data.

Source: U.S. Department of Justice, Bureau of Justice Statistics, School Crime Supplement (SCS) to the National Crime Victimization Survey, 2001.

Table 5. Percentage of students ages 12–18 who reported avoiding certain areas of school and skipping school, class, or extracurricular activities during the previous 6 months, by reports of being bullied directly and/or indirectly at school: 2001

Victim behaviors	Number of students	Avoided shortest route	Avoided entrance to school	Avoided hallways or stairs	Avoided school cafeteria	Avoided restrooms	Avoided other places in school building	Avoided parking lot	Avoided other places on school grounds	Skipped school	Skipped class	Skipped extra-curricular activities
Total	24,315,000	2.5	1.2	2.1	1.4	2.2	1.4	1.6	1.7	1.1	0.6	1.1
Not Bullied	20,680,000	1.9	0.8	1.3	0.7	1.5	0.8	1.1	1.1	0.7	0.2	0.6
Bullied	3,494,000	5.9	3.6	7.1	5.8	6.9	5.3	5.0	5.5	3.8	3.0	3.8
Both Directly												
and Indirectly[1]	1,095,000	9.3	6.6	12.2	9.8	10.4	9.4	7.5	9.4	7.2	6.5	6.0
Directly Only[1]	816,000	3.4	2.7	7.5	5.0	6.2	4.8	4.7	5.3	4.3	2.5	4.2
Indirectly Only[1]	1,583,000	4.9	2.0	3.4	3.4	4.8	2.8	3.4	2.8	1.3	0.8	2.1

[1] Categories are mutually exclusive.

Note: "At school" was defined as in the school building, on school property, on a school bus, or going to and from school. Youth ages 12 through 18 were first asked if "they had been bullied at school. That is, had anyone picked on them a lot or tried to make them do things they did not want to do (e.g., give them money)?" This is referred to as direct bullying. They were also asked, "Have you felt rejected because other students have made fun of you, called you names, or excluded you from activities?" This is referred to as indirect bullying. Total bullied includes youth who reported they were bullied directly or indirectly. Population size for students ages 12–18 is 24,315,000. Detail may not sum to totals due to missing data.

Source: U.S. Department of Justice, Bureau of Justice Statistics, School Crime Supplement (SCS) to the National Crime Victimization Survey, 2001.

Table 6. Percentage of students ages 12–18 who reported carrying a weapon for protection or being involved in a physical fight at school during the previous 6 months, by reports of being bullied directly and/or indirectly at school: 2001

Victim behaviors	Number of students	Carried a weapon	Involved in a physical fight
Total	24,315,000	1.8	5.2
Not Bullied	20,680,000	1.4	3.6
Bullied	3,494,000	3.7	14.6
Both Directly and Indirectly[1]	1,095,000	4.4	21.1
Directly Only[1]	816,000	3.3	15.0
Indirectly Only[1]	1,583,000	3.4	9.8

[1] Categories are mutually exclusive.

Note: Students included as carrying weapons reported carrying a gun, knife or other weapon to school in the 6 months prior to the survey. "At school" includes inside the school building, on school property, or on the way to or from school. Youth ages 12 through 18 were first asked if "they had been bullied at school. That is, had anyone picked on them a lot or tried to make them do things they did not want to do (e.g., give them money)?" This is referred to as direct bullying. They were also asked, "Have you felt rejected because other students have made fun of you, called you names, or excluded you from activities?" This is referred to as indirect bullying. Total bullied includes youth who reported they were bullied directly or indirectly. Population size for students ages 12–18 is 24,315,000. Detail may not sum to totals due to missing data.

Source: U.S. Department of Justice, Bureau of Justice Statistics, School Crime Supplement (SCS) to the National Crime Victimization Survey, 2001.

Table 7. Percentage of students ages 12–18 who reported receiving different academic grades during the school year, by reports of being bullied directly and/or indirectly at school: 2001

	Number of students	Self-reports of grades			
		Mostly A's	Mostly B's	Mostly C's	Mostly D's and F's
Total	24,315,000	32.6	40.8	20.8	3.9
Not Bullied	20,680,000	33.7	41.0	20.4	3.2
Bullied	3,494,000	26.6	40.6	23.7	8.3
Both Directly and Indirectly[1]	1,095,000	21.2	38.6	26.7	12.1
Directly Only[1]	816,000	26.5	39.4	26.7	7.1
Indirectly Only[1]	1,583,000	30.3	42.5	20.1	6.3

[1] Categories are mutually exclusive.

Note: "At school" includes inside the school building, on school property, or on the way to or from school. Youth ages 12 through 18 were first asked if "they had been bullied at school. That is, had anyone picked on them a lot or tried to make them do things they did not want to do (e.g., give them money)?" This is referred to as direct bullying. They were also asked, "Have you felt rejected because other students have made fun of you, called you names, or excluded you from activities?" This is referred to as indirect bullying. Total bullied includes youth who reported they were bullied directly or indirectly. Population size for students ages 12–18 is 24,315,000. Detail may not sum to totals due to missing data.

Source: U.S. Department of Justice, Bureau of Justice Statistics, School Crime Supplement (SCS) to the National Crime Victimization Survey, 2001.

APPENDIX C: STANDARD ERROR TABLES

Table S1. Standard errors Table 1. Percentage of students ages 12–18 who reported being bullied directly and/or indirectly at school during the previous 6 months, by selected student characteristics: 2001

Student Characteristics	Bullied			
	Total	Both Directly and Indirectly	Directly Only	Indirectly Only
Total	0.54	0.23	0.22	0.37
Student sex				
Male	0.72	0.35	0.36	0.45
Female	0.62	0.32	0.28	0.43

Table S1. (cont.)

Student Characteristics	Bullied			
	Total	Both Directly and Indirectly	Directly Only	Indirectly Only
Student race/ethnicity				
White, non-Hispanic	0.63	0.31	0.27	0.45
Black, non-Hispanic	1.32	0.54	0.60	0.86
Hispanic	1.16	0.68	0.42	0.70
Other, non-Hispanic	1.72	0.86	0.84	1.08
Student grade				
Sixth	1.59	0.98	0.90	1.23
Seventh	1.33	0.75	0.58	1.01
Eighth	1.12	0.60	0.53	0.73
Ninth	1.02	0.55	0.71	0.65
Tenth	0.90	0.42	0.45	0.78
Eleventh	0.80	0.53	0.28	0.70
Twelfth	0.99	0.32	0.43	0.83
Student household income				
Less than $7,500	2.29	1.13	1.12	1.73
$7,500–14,999	2.33	1.20	1.08	1.61
$15,000–24,999	1.73	1.00	0.76	1.13
$25,000–34,999	1.29	0.74	0.77	0.74
$35,000–49,999	1.11	0.55	0.49	0.84
$50,000–74,999	0.94	0.56	0.41	0.68
$75,000 or more	0.91	0.50	0.39	0.63
Student place of residence				
Urban	0.82	0.44	0.37	0.54
Suburban	0.65	0.32	0.26	0.45
Rural	1.63	0.57	0.69	1.01

Note: "At school" was defined as in the school building, on school property, on a school bus, or going to and from school. Youth ages 12 through 18 were first asked if "they had been bullied at school. That is, had anyone picked on them a lot or tried to make them do things they did not want to do (e.g., give them money)?" This is referred to as direct bullying. They were also asked, "Have you felt rejected because other students have made fun of you, called you names, or excluded you from activities?" This is referred to as indirect bullying. Total bullied includes youth who reported they were bullied directly or indirectly. Population size for students ages 12–18 is 24,315,000.

Source: U.S. Department of Justice, Bureau of Justice Statistics, School Crime Supplement (SCS) to the National Crime Victimization Survey, 2001.

Table S2. Standard errors for Table 2. Percentage of students ages 12–18 who reported being bullied directly and/or indirectly at school during the previous 6 months, by selected school characteristics: 2001

School Characteristics	Bullied			
	Total	Both Directly and Indirectly	Directly Only	Indirectly Only
Total	0.54	0.23	0.22	0.37
School type				
Public	0.56	0.89	0.23	0.39
Private	1.18	0.23	0.68	0.87
Gang presence				
Yes	1.13	0.70	0.52	0.73
No	0.57	0.26	0.28	0.42
Presence of security officers or assigned police				
Yes	0.60	0.27	0.30	0.41
No	0.86	0.45	0.33	0.64
Hallway supervision by school staff				
Yes	0.53	0.23	0.23	0.36
No	1.31	0.82	0.57	1.01

Note: "At school" includes inside the school building, on school property, or on the way to or from school. Youth ages 12 through 18 were first asked if "they had been bullied at school. That is, had anyone picked on them a lot or tried to make them do things they did not want to do (e.g., give them money)?" This is referred to as direct bullying. They were also asked, "Have you felt rejected because other students have made fun of you, called you names, or excluded you from activities?" This is referred to as indirect bullying. Total bullied includes youth who reported they were bullied directly or indirectly. Population size for students ages 12–18 is 24,315,000.

Source: U.S. Department of Justice, Bureau of Justice Statistics, School Crime Supplement (SCS) to the National Crime Victimization Survey, 2001.

Table S3. Standard Errors for Table 3. Percentage of students ages 12–18 who reported being victimized at school during the previous 6 months, by reports of being bullied directly and/or indirectly at school: 2001

	Victimization			
	Any	**Serious Violent**	**Violent**	**Property**
Total	0.31	0.08	0.19	0.24
Not Bullied	0.27	0.06	0.10	0.24
Bullied	1.13	0.41	0.94	0.78
Both Directly and Indirectly	2.19	1.20	2.03	1.63
Directly Only	2.47	0.46	2.01	1.64
Indirectly Only	1.26	0.23	0.89	1.09

Note: Serious violent crimes include rape, sexual assault, robbery, and aggravated assault. Violent crimes include serious violent crimes and simple assault. Any crimes include violent crimes and theft. "At school" includes inside the school building, on school property, or on the way to or from school. Youth ages 12 through 18 were first asked if "they had been bullied at school. That is, had anyone picked on them a lot or tried to make them do things they did not want to do (e.g., give them money)?" This is referred to as direct bullying. They were also asked, "Have you felt rejected because other students have made fun of you, called you names, or excluded you from activities?" This is referred to as indirect bullying. Total bullied includes youth who reported they were bullied directly or indirectly. Population size for students ages 12–18 is 24,315,000.

Source: U.S. Department of Justice, Bureau of Justice Statistics, School Crime Supplement (SCS) to the National Crime Victimization Survey, 2001.

Table S4. Standard errors for Table 4. Percentage of students ages 12–18 who reported fearing attack during the previous 6 months at school, on the way to and from school, and away from school, by reports of being bullied directly and/or indirectly at school: 2001

Victim behaviors	Afraid of attack at school			Afraid of attack on the way to or from school			Afraid of attack away from school		
	Never	Almost Never	Sometimes/ Most of the Time	Never	Almost Never	Sometimes/ Most of the Time	Never	Almost Never	Sometimes/ Most of the Time
Total	0.62	0.55	0.29	0.44	0.35	0.24	0.60	0.52	0.28
Not Bullied	0.53	0.48	0.23	0.44	0.38	0.23	0.62	0.53	0.26
Bullied	1.84	1.82	1.35	1.30	1.15	0.94	1.52	1.34	1.08
Both Directly and Indirectly	2.77	2.39	2.63	2.61	2.13	2.09	2.34	2.19	1.90
Directly Only	3.53	3.55	2.28	2.83	2.39	1.83	3.57	3.70	2.02
Indirectly Only	2.69	2.57	1.56	1.76	1.51	1.00	2.10	1.63	1.65

Note: "At school" was defined as in the school building, on school property, on a school bus, or going to and from school. Youth ages 12 through 18 were first asked if "they had been bullied at school. That is, had anyone picked on them a lot or tried to make them do things they did not want to do (e.g., give them money)?" This is referred to as direct bullying. They were also asked, "Have you felt rejected because other students have made fun of you, called you names, or excluded you from activities?" This is referred to as indirect bullying. Total bullied includes youth who reported they were bullied directly or indirectly. Population size for students ages 12–18 is 24,315,000.

Source: U.S. Department of Justice, Bureau of Justice Statistics, School Crime Supplement (SCS) to the National Crime Victimization Survey, 2001.

Table S5. Standard errors for Table 5. Percentage of students ages 12–18 who reported avoiding certain areas of school and skipping school, class, or extra-curricular activities during the previous 6 months, by reports of being bullied directly and/or indirectly at school: 2001

Victim behaviors	Avoided shortest route	Avoided entrance to school	Avoided hallways or stairs	Avoided school cafeteria	Avoided restrooms	Avoided other places in school building	Avoided parking lot	Avoided other places on school grounds	Skipped school	Skipped class	Skipped extra-curricular activities
Total	0.20	0.11	0.18	0.16	0.19	0.14	0.14	0.15	0.13	0.09	0.12
Not Bullied	0.17	0.11	0.15	0.11	0.16	0.11	0.12	0.12	0.11	0.06	0.10
Bullied	0.82	0.56	0.81	0.75	0.74	0.71	0.57	0.70	0.66	0.53	0.48
Both Directly											
and Indirectly	1.61	1.28	1.80	1.78	1.59	1.64	1.31	1.56	1.59	1.42	1.18
Directly Only	1.11	1.05	1.63	1.35	1.38	1.27	1.28	1.47	1.00	0.84	1.00
Indirectly Only	1.17	0.57	0.82	0.82	0.98	0.76	0.75	0.68	0.60	0.46	0.66

Note: "At school" was defined as in the school building, on school property, on a school bus, or going to and from school. Youth ages 12 through 18 were first asked if "they had been bullied at school. That is, had anyone picked on them a lot or tried to make them do things they did not want to do (e.g., give them money)?" This is referred to as direct bullying. They were also asked, "Have you felt rejected because other students have made fun of you, called you names, or excluded you from activities?" This is referred to as indirect bullying. Total bullied includes youth who reported they were bullied directly or indirectly. Population size for students ages 12–18 is 24,315,000.

Source: U.S. Department of Justice, Bureau of Justice Statistics, School Crime Supplement (SCS) to the National Crime Victimization Survey, 2001.

Table S6. Standard errors for Table 6. Percentage of students ages 12–18 who reported carrying a weapon for protection or being involved in a physical fight at school during the previous 6 months, by reports of being bullied directly and/or indirectly at school: 2001

Victim behaviors	Carried a weapon	Involved in a physical fight
Total	0.19	0.26
Not Bullied	0.18	0.22
Bullied	0.69	1.12
Both Directly and Indirectly	1.08	2.06
Directly Only	1.18	2.38
Indirectly Only	0.96	1.44

Note: Students included as carrying weapons reported carrying a gun, knife or other weapon to school in the 6 months prior to the survey. "At school" includes inside the school building, on school property, or on the way to or from school. Youth ages 12 through 18 were first asked if "they had been bullied at school. That is, had anyone picked on them a lot or tried to make them do things they did not want to do (e.g., give them money)?" This is referred to as direct bullying. They were also asked, "Have you felt rejected because other students have made fun of you, called you names, or excluded you from activities?" This is referred to as indirect bullying. Total bullied includes youth who reported they were bullied directly or indirectly. Population size for students ages 12–18 is 24,315,000.

Source: U.S. Department of Justice, Bureau of Justice Statistics, School Crime Supplement (SCS) to the National Crime Victimization Survey, 2001.

Table S7. Standard errors for Table 7. Percentage of students ages 12–18 who reported receiving different academic grades during the school year, by reports of being bullied directly and/or indirectly at school: 2001

	Self-reports of grades			
	Mostly A's	**Mostly B's**	**Mostly C's**	**Mostly D's and F's**
Total	0.69	0.64	0.55	0.26
Not Bullied	0.72	0.68	0.59	0.24
Bullied	1.35	1.50	1.41	0.93
Both Directly and Indirectly	2.35	2.66	2.53	1.66
Directly Only	3.36	2.95	3.18	1.53
Indirectly Only	2.19	2.39	1.82	1.35

Note: "At school" includes inside the school building, on school property, or on the way to or from school. Youth ages 12 through 18 were first asked if "they had been bullied at school. That is, had anyone picked on them a lot or tried to make them do things they did not want to do (e.g., give them money)?" This is referred to as direct bullying. They were also asked, "Have you felt rejected because other students have made fun of you, called you names, or excluded you from activities?" This is referred to as indirect bullying. Total bullied includes youth who reported they were bullied directly or indirectly. Population size for students ages 12–18 is 24,315,000.

Source: U.S. Department of Justice, Bureau of Justice Statistics, School Crime Supplement (SCS) to the National Crime Victimization Survey, 2001.

APPENDIX D: 2001 SCHOOL CRIME SUPPLEMENT TO THE NATIONAL CRIME VICTIMIZATION SURVEY INSTRUMENT

OMB No. 1121-0184: Approval Expires 11/30/2001

NOTICE – We are conducting this survey under the authority of Title 13, United States Code, Section 8. Section 9 of this law requires us to keep all information about you and your household strictly confidential. We may use this information only for statistical purposes. Also, Title 42, Section 3732, United States Code, authorizes the Bureau of Justice Statistics, Department of Justice, to collect information using this survey. Title 42, Sections 3789g and 3735, United States Code also requires us to keep all information about you and your household strictly confidential.

ASK OF ALL PERSONS 12–18.

FORM SCS-1 (10-31-2000)

U.S. DEPARTMENT OF COMMERCE
Economics and Statistics Administration
U.S. CENSUS BUREAU
ACTING AS COLLECTING AGENT FOR THE BUREAU OF JUSTICE STATISTICS
U.S. DEPARTMENT OF JUSTICE

We estimate that it will take from 5 to 15 minutes to complete this interview with 10 minutes being the average time. If you have any comments regarding these estimates or any other aspect of this survey, send them to the Associate Director for Finance and Administration, Room 2027, U.S. Census Bureau, Washington DC 20233, or to the Office of Information and Regulatory Affairs, Office of Management and Budget, Washington, DC 20503. According to the Paperwork Reduction Act of 1995, no persons are required to respond to a collection of information unless such collection displays a valid OMB control number.

SCHOOL CRIME SUPPLEMENT TO THE NATIONAL CRIME VICTIMIZATION SURVEY 2001

Sample: J____ | **Control number**: PSU | Segment | CK | Serial

A. FR code: 001

B. Respondent: Line No. 002 | Age 003 | Name

FIELD REPRESENTATIVE – *Complete an SCS-1 form for all persons 12-18 in all interviewed households even when that person is a Type Z noninterview. Do NOT complete an SCS-1 form for persons 12-18 if the household is a Type A.*

C. Type of SCS Interview

004
1☐ Personal – Self
2☐ Telephone – Self
3☐ Personal – Proxy
4☐ Telephone – Proxy
(1–4: ***SKIP*** to INTRO 1)
5☐ Noninterview – *FILL ITEM D*

D. Reason for SCS noninterview

005 1☐ Type Z noninterview on NCVS

SCS noninterview
2☐ Refused
3☐ Not available
4☐ Physically or mentally unable and no proxy available

FIELD REPRESENTATIVE –*Read introduction.*

INTRO 1 – **Now I have some additional questions about your school. These answers will be kept confidential, by law.**

E. SCREEN QUESTIONS FOR SUPPLEMENT

1a. Did you attend school at any time during the last 6 months, that is, any time since ____________ 1st?

006
1☐ Yes
2☐ No – *END INTERVIEW*

1b. During that time, were you ever home-schooled? That is, did you receive ANY of that schooling at home, rather than in a public or private school?

092
1☐ Yes
2☐ No –***SKIP*** to 2b

1c. Was ALL or SOME of that home schooling?

007
1☐ All –*END INTERVIEW*
2☐ Some

2a. During the last 6 months, that is, any time since ____________ 1st, if you were in a public or private school, what grade would you be in?

093
0☐ Fifth or under – *END INTERVIEW*

1☐ Sixth
2☐ Seventh
3☐ Eighth
4☐ Ninth
5☐ Tenth
6☐ Eleventh
7☐ Twelfth
8☐ Other –*Specify*____________
(1–8: ***SKIP*** to INTRO 2)

9☐ College/GED/Post-graduate/ Other noneligible – *END INTERVIEW*

2b. During the last 6 months, that is, any time since ____________ 1st, what grade were you in school?

008
0☐ Fifth or under – *END INTERVIEW*

1☐ Sixth
2☐ Seventh
3☐ Eighth
4☐ Ninth
5☐ Tenth
6☐ Eleventh
7☐ Twelfth
8☐ Other –*Specify*____________
(1–8: ***SKIP*** to 3)

9☐ College/GED/Post-graduate/ Other noneligible – *END INTERVIEW*

E. SCREEN QUESTIONS FOR SUPPLEMENT – Continued

FIELD REPRESENTATIVE –*Read introduction only if any of the boxes 1–8 are marked in item 2a.*

INTRO 2 – **The following questions pertain only to your attendance at a public or private school and not to being home-schooled.**

3. In what month did your current school year begin?	009	1☐ August 2☐ September 3☐ Other – *Specify*
4. Did you attend school for all of the last 6 months?	010	1☐ Yes –***SKIP*** to 6a 2☐ No
5. How many months were you in school during the last 6 months?	011	1☐ One month 2☐ Two months 3☐ Three months 4☐ Four months 5☐ Five months

F. ENVIRONMENTAL QUESTIONS

6a. What is the complete name of your school?	012	Office Use Only
6b. In what city, county, and state is your school located? FIELD REPRESENTATIVE –*Probe, if necessary.*	013	City County
	014	Office Use Only State
	015	Office Use Only
7a. Is your school public or private?	016	1☐ Public –*ASK 7b* 2☐ Private –***SKIP*** to 7c
7b. Is this your regularly assigned school or a school that you or your family chose?	017	1☐ Assigned 2☐ Chosen 3☐ Assigned school is school of choice } ***SKIP*** to 8
7c. Is your school church-related?	018	1☐ Yes –*ASK 7d* 2☐ No –***SKIP*** to 8 3☐ Don't know –*ASK 7d*
7d. Is your school Catholic?	019	1☐ Yes, Catholic 2☐ No, other religion
8. What grades are taught in your school? Pre-K or Kindergarten 00 01 02 03 04 05 06 07 08 09 10 11 12 H.S. Senior 13 Post-graduate 20 All ungraded 30 All Special Education	020 021	Grades: (lowest) TO (highest)
9. How do you get to school most of the time? FIELD REPRESENTATIVE – *If multiple modes are used, code the mode in which the student spends the most time.*	022	1☐ Walk 2☐ School bus 3☐ Public bus, subway, train 4☐ Car 5☐ Bicycle, motorbike, or motorcycle 6☐ Some other way –*Specify*

Page 2 FORM SCS-1 (10-31-2000)

F. ENVIRONMENTAL QUESTIONS – Continued

10. How long does it take you to get from your home to school most of the time?

023
- 1 ☐ Less than 15 minutes
- 2 ☐ 15-29 minutes
- 3 ☐ 30-44 minutes
- 4 ☐ 45-59 minutes
- 5 ☐ 60 minutes or longer

11. How do you get home from school most of the time?

FIELD REPRESENTATIVE – *If multiple modes are used, code the mode in which the student spends the most time.*

If the student volunteers that he or she does not go directly home after school, record the mode that the student uses to get to his or her first destination after school.

024
- 1 ☐ Walk
- 2 ☐ School bus
- 3 ☐ Public bus, subway, train
- 4 ☐ Car
- 5 ☐ Bicycle, motorbike, or motorcycle
- 6 ☐ Some other way – *Specify* ↙ ______________________

12a. Are most students at your school allowed to leave the school grounds to eat lunch?

025
- 1 ☐ Yes
- 2 ☐ No
- 3 ☐ Don't know

12b. How often do you leave school grounds at lunch time?

(READ CATEGORIES.)

026
- 1 ☐ **Never**
- 2 ☐ **Once or twice a year**
- 3 ☐ **Once or twice a month**
- 4 ☐ **Once or twice a week**
- 5 ☐ **Almost every day**

13. During the last 6 months, have you participated in any extra-curricular activities sponsored by your school?

027
- 1 ☐ Yes
- 2 ☐ No

14. Does your school take any measures to ensure the safety of students?

For example, does the school have:

		Yes	No	DK
a. Security guards and/or assigned police officers?	028	1 ☐	2 ☐	3 ☐
b. Other school staff or other adults supervising the hallway?	029	1 ☐	2 ☐	3 ☐
c. Metal detectors?	030	1 ☐	2 ☐	3 ☐
d. Locked entrance or exit doors during the day?	031	1 ☐	2 ☐	3 ☐
e. A requirement that visitors sign in?	032	1 ☐	2 ☐	3 ☐
f. Locker checks?	033	1 ☐	2 ☐	3 ☐
g. A requirement that students wear badges or picture identification?	094	1 ☐	2 ☐	3 ☐
h. One or more security cameras to monitor the school?	095	1 ☐	2 ☐	3 ☐
i. A code of student conduct, that is, a set of written rules or guidelines that the school provides you?	096	1 ☐	2 ☐	3 ☐

15. I am going to read a list of statements that could describe a school. Thinking about your school over the last 6 months, would you strongly agree, agree, disagree, or strongly disagree with the following...

		Strongly Agree	Agree	Disagree	Strongly Disagree
a. Everyone knows what the school rules are	034	1 ☐	2 ☐	3 ☐	4 ☐
b. The school rules are fair	035	1 ☐	2 ☐	3 ☐	4 ☐
c. The punishment for breaking school rules is the same no matter who you are	036	1 ☐	2 ☐	3 ☐	4 ☐
d. The school rules are strictly enforced	037	1 ☐	2 ☐	3 ☐	4 ☐
e. If a school rule is broken, students know what kind of punishment will follow	038	1 ☐	2 ☐	3 ☐	4 ☐

16. During the last 6 months, that is, since ______________ 1st, have you attended any drug education classes in your school?

039
- 1 ☐ Yes
- 2 ☐ No
- 3 ☐ Don't know

FORM SCS-1 (10-31-2000)

Page 3

F. ENVIRONMENTAL QUESTIONS – Continued

FIELD REPRESENTATIVE –*Read introduction.*

INTRO 3 – **Now I have some more questions about things that happened at school. For this survey, "at school" includes the school building, on school property, on a school bus, or going to and from school. I want to remind you that all of your answers are confidential.**

17a. The following question refers to the availability of drugs and alcohol at your school.

Tell me if you don't know what any of these items are.

FIELD REPRESENTATIVE – *For each item ask,*

Is it possible to get ______ at your school?

		Yes	No	DK	DK drug
a. **Alcoholic beverages**	040	1☐	2☐	3☐	4☐
b. **Marijuana**	041	1☐	2☐	3☐	4☐
c. **Crack**	042	1☐	2☐	3☐	4☐
d. **Other forms of cocaine**	043	1☐	2☐	3☐	4☐
e. **Uppers such as ecstasy, crystal meth, or other illegal stimulants**	097	1☐	2☐	3☐	4☐
f. **Downers such as GHB or sleeping pills**	098	1☐	2☐	3☐	4☐
g. **LSD or acid**	045	1☐	2☐	3☐	4☐
h. **PCP or angel dust**	046	1☐	2☐	3☐	4☐
i. **Heroin or smack**	047	1☐	2☐	3☐	4☐
j. **Other illegal drugs –** *If "Yes" is marked, ASK* –**What drugs?** *(Exclude tobacco products.)*	048	1☐ Specify ______	2☐	3☐	4☐

FIELD REPRESENTATIVE –*Refer to Drug Slang Cards (SCS-2a and SCS-2b). Reclassify the "other illegal drug(s)" to one of the categories a-i if possible. If able to reclassify the drug(s) mentioned, mark the "No" box in category j, otherwise, mark the "Yes" box in category j and enter the "other illegal drug(s)" mentioned in the Specify space.*

17b. FIELD REPRESENTATIVE –*For each YES response in 17a ask the drug, otherwise mark NA for each category not marked YES in 17a.*

Would you say ______ (is/are) easy, fairly easy, fairly hard, or hard to get at your school?

		Easy	Fairly Easy	Fairly Hard	Hard	NA
a. **Alcoholic beverages**	049	1☐	2☐	3☐	4☐	5☐
b. **Marijuana**	050	1☐	2☐	3☐	4☐	5☐
c. **Crack**	051	1☐	2☐	3☐	4☐	5☐
d. **Other forms of cocaine**	052	1☐	2☐	3☐	4☐	5☐
e. **Uppers such as ecstasy, crystal meth, or other illegal stimulants**	099	1☐	2☐	3☐	4☐	5☐
f. **Downers such as GHB or sleeping pills**	100	1☐	2☐	3☐	4☐	5☐
g. **LSD or acid**	054	1☐	2☐	3☐	4☐	5☐
h. **PCP or angel dust**	055	1☐	2☐	3☐	4☐	5☐
i. **Heroin or smack**	056	1☐	2☐	3☐	4☐	5☐
j. **Other illegal drugs**	057	1☐	2☐	3☐	4☐	5☐

17c. During the last 6 months, did you know for sure that any students were on drugs or alcohol while they were at school? | 101 | 1☐ Yes 2☐ No

17d. During the last 6 months, did anyone offer, or try to sell or give you an illegal drug other than alcohol or tobacco at your school? | 102 | 1☐ Yes 2☐ No

G. FIGHTING, BULLYING AND HATE BEHAVIORS

18a. During the last 6 months, have you been in one or more physical fights at school? | 103 | 1☐ Yes 2☐ No –***SKIP*** to 19

18b. During the last 6 months, how many times have you been in a physical fight at school? | 104 | ☐☐☐ (Number of times)

Page 4 FORM SCS-1 (10-31-2000)

G. FIGHTING, BULLYING AND HATE BEHAVIORS – Continued

19. During the last 6 months, have you been bullied at school? That is, has anyone picked on you a lot or tried to make you do things you didn't want to do like give them money? (You may include incidents you reported before.)

067 ₁☐ Yes ₂☐ No

20a. During the last 6 months, have you often felt rejected by other students at school? For example, have you felt rejected because other students have made fun of you, called you names, or excluded you from activities?

105 ₁☐ Yes ₂☐ No – ***SKIP*** to 21a

20b. During the last 6 months, how often have you been made fun of, called names, or excluded from activities?

(READ CATEGORIES.)

106
₁☐ **Once or twice in the last 6 months**
₂☐ **Once or twice a month**
₃☐ **Once or twice a week, or**
₄☐ **Almost every day**

21a. During the last 6 months, has anyone called you a derogatory or bad name at school having to do with your race, religion, ethnic background or national origin, disability, gender, or sexual orientation? We call these hate-related words.

065 ₁☐ Yes ₂☐ No – ***SKIP*** to 22

21b. Were any of the hate-related words related to ...

		Yes	No	DK
a. Your race?	107	₁☐	₂☐	₃☐
b. Your religion?	108	₁☐	₂☐	₃☐
c. Your ethnic background or national origin (for example people of Hispanic origin)?	109	₁☐	₂☐	₃☐
d. Any disability (by this I mean physical, mental, or developmental disabilities) you may have?	110	₁☐	₂☐	₃☐
e. Your gender?	111	₁☐	₂☐	₃☐
f. Your sexual orientation?	112	₁☐	₂☐	₃☐

If "Yes," SAY –**(by this I mean homosexual, bisexual, or heterosexual)**

22. During the last 6 months, have you seen any hate-related words or symbols written in school classrooms, school bathrooms, school hallways, or on the outside of your school building?

066 ₁☐ Yes ₂☐ No

H. AVOIDANCE

23a. During the last 6 months, that is, since ________ 1st, did you STAY AWAY from any of the following places because you thought someone might attack or threaten to attack you there?

(READ CATEGORIES.)

		Yes	No
a. The shortest route to school?	068	₁☐	₂☐
b. The entrance into the school?	069	₁☐	₂☐
c. Any hallways or stairs in school?	070	₁☐	₂☐
d. Parts of the school cafeteria?	071	₁☐	₂☐
e. Any school restrooms?	072	₁☐	₂☐
f. Other places inside the school building?	073	₁☐	₂☐
g. School parking lot?	074	₁☐	₂☐
h. Other places on school grounds?	075	₁☐	₂☐

23b. Did you AVOID any extra-curricular activities at your school because you thought someone might attack or threaten to attack you?

076 ₁☐ Yes ₂☐ No

FORM SCS-1 (10-31-2000) Page 5

H. AVOIDANCE - Continued

Question	Item	Response
23c. Did you AVOID any classes because you thought someone might attack or threaten to attack you?	077	1☐Yes 2☐No
23d. Did you stay home from school because you thought someone might attack or threaten to attack you at school, or going to or from school?	078	1☐Yes 2☐No
24. How often are you afraid that someone will attack or threaten to attack you at school? *(READ CATEGORIES.)*	079	1☐ **Never** 2☐ **Almost never** 3☐ **Sometimes** 4☐ **Most of the time**
25. How often are you afraid that someone will attack or threaten to attack you on the way to and from school? *(READ CATEGORIES.)*	080	1☐ **Never** 2☐ **Almost never** 3☐ **Sometimes** 4☐ **Most of the time**
26. Besides the times you are at school, or going to or from school, how often are you afraid that someone will attack or threaten to attack you? *(READ CATEGORIES.)*	081	1☐ **Never** 2☐ **Almost never** 3☐ **Sometimes** 4☐ **Most of the time**

I. WEAPONS

Question	Item	Response
27a. Some people bring guns, knives or objects that can be used as weapons to school for protection. During the last 6 months, that is, since ______ 1st, did you ever bring a gun to school or onto school grounds?	082	1☐Yes 2☐No
27b. During the last 6 months, did you ever bring a knife to school or onto school grounds? Include only knives brought as weapons.	083	1☐Yes 2☐No
27c. During the last 6 months, did you ever bring some other weapon to school or onto school grounds?	084	1☐Yes 2☐No
28a. Do you know any (other) students who have brought a gun to your school in the last 6 months?	085	1☐Yes 2☐No
28b. Have you actually seen another student with a gun at school in the last 6 months?	086	1☐Yes 2☐No 3☐Don't know
29. During the last 6 months, could you have gotten a loaded gun without adult supervision, either at school or away from school?	113	1☐Yes 2☐No

J. GANGS

FIELD REPRESENTATIVE –*Read introduction.*

INTRO 4 – **We'd like to know about gangs at your school. You may know these as street gangs, fighting gangs, crews, or something else. Gangs may use common names, signs, symbols, or colors. For this survey, we are interested in all gangs, whether or not they are involved in violent or illegal activity.**

Question	Item	Response
30. Are there any gangs at your school?	058	1☐Yes 2☐No 3☐Don't know
31. During the last 6 months, that is, since ______ 1st, how often have gangs been involved in fights, attacks, or other violence at your school? *(READ CATEGORIES 1–5.)*	089	1☐**Never** 2☐**Once or twice in the last 6 months** 3☐**Once or twice a month** 4☐**Once or twice a week, or** 5☐**Almost every day** 6☐Don't know
32. Have gangs been involved in the sale of drugs at your school in the last 6 months?	090	1☐Yes 2☐No 3☐Don't know

Page 6 FORM SCS-1 (10-31-2000)

K. STUDENT CHARACTERISTICS

33a. During the last 4 weeks, did you skip any classes?	114	1☐ Yes 2☐ No – ***SKIP*** to 34 3☐ Don't know – ***SKIP*** to 34
33b. During the last 4 weeks, on how many days did you skip at least one class?	115	☐☐ (Number of days)
34. During this school year, across all subjects have you gotten mostly - *(READ CATEGORIES 1-5.)*	116	1☐ A's 2☐ B's 3☐ C's 4☐ D's 5☐ F's 6☐ School does not give grades/no alphabetic grade equivalent

35. Thinking about the future, do you think you will....

		Yes	No	DK
a. Attend school after high school?	117	1☐	2☐ – ***SKIP*** to CHECK ITEM A	3☐
b. Graduate from a 4-year college?	118	1☐	2☐	3☐

CHECK ITEM A	Were the supplement questions asked in private, or was an adult member of the household or family present during at least part of the questions? *If not sure or if a telephone interview, ask –* **Was an adult member of the household or family present during at least part of these questions?**	091	1☐ **Personal interview** – No adult present 2☐ **Personal interview** – Adult present 3☐ **Telephone interview** – No adult present 4☐ **Telephone interview** – Adult present 5☐ **Telephone interview** – Don't know
CHECK ITEM B	Is this the last household member to be interviewed?		☐ Yes – END SUPPLEMENT ☐ No – Interview next household member

FORM SCS-1 (10-31-2000)

ACKNOWLEDGMENTS

The School Crime Supplement to the National Crime Victimization Survey would not be possible without the continued support for data collection given by the U.S. Department of Education, Office of Safe and Drug-free Schools under the sponsorship of Bill Modzeleski.

Staff from the National Center for Education Statistics provided valuable comments and suggestions on drafts of this study, including Jeffrey Owings, Tai Phan, Marilyn Seastrom, Marilyn Binkley, and Carl Schmitt. In addition, Ann Ricciuti of the Institute for Education Sciences gathered and mediated comments from two anonymous external reviewers that greatly improved this article.

The authors would like to acknowledge Mike Planty, Sally Ruddy, Amanda Miller, Margaret Noonan, and Martin Hahn of the American Institutes for Research, Education Statistics Services Institute (ESSI), for their comments and guidance. Finally, the authors are grateful to Elina Hartwell, also from ESSI, for the artful production and layout of this study.

REFERENCES

Addington, L.A., Ruddy, S.A., Miller, A.K., and DeVoe, J.F. (2002). *Are America's Schools Safe? Students Speak Out: 1999 School Crime Supplement* (NCES 2002–331). U.S. Department of Education, National Center for Education Statistics. Washington, DC: U.S. Government Printing Office.

Banks, R. (1997). *Bullying in Schools*. Office of Educational Research and Improvement. U.S. Department of Education, ERIC: Washington DC: U.S. Government Printing Office

Bastian, L. and Taylor, B. (1991). *School Crime 1991* (NCJ 131645). U.S. Department of Justice, Office of Justice Programs, Bureau of Justice Statistics. Washington, DC: U.S. Government Printing Office.

Batsche, G. M. and Knoff, H. M. (1994). Bullies and their Victims: Understanding a Pervasive Problem in the Schools. *School Psychology Review, 23*: 165-174.

Berthhold, K. and Hoover, J. (2000). Correlates of Bullying and Victimization Among Intermediate Students in the Midwestern USA. *School Psychology International*, *21*: 65–79.

Cairns, R.B., Cairns, B.D., Neckerman, H.G., Ferguson, L.L., and Gariepy, J. (1989). Growth and Aggression: 1. Childhood to Early Adolescence. *Developmental Psychology, 25*: 320-330.

Cantor, D. and Lynch, J. P. (2000). Self-Report Surveys as Measures of Crime and Criminal Victimization. In David Duffee (Ed.), *Measurement and Analysis of Crime and Justice*. Washington, DC: National Institute of Justice.

Carney, A. and Merrell, K. (2001). Bullying in Schools: Perspectives on Understanding and Preventing an International Problem. *School Psychology International, 21*: 364–382.

Cillessen, A.H.N., and Mayeux, L. (2004). From Censure to Reinforcement: Developmental Changes in the Association Between Aggression and Social Status. *Child Development, 75*: 147–163.

Crick, N.R., and Grotpeter, J.K. (1995). Relational Aggression, Gender, and Social-psychological Adjustment. *Child Development, 66*: 710–722.

DeVoe, J.F., Peter, K., Kaufman, P., Miller, A.K., Noonan, M., Snyder, T.D., and Baum, K. *Indicators of School Crime and Safety: 2004*. NCES 2005–002/NCJ 205290. U.S. Departments of Education and Justice. Washington, DC: 2004.

Dodge, K., Coie, J., Pettit, G.S., and Price, J. (1990). Peer Status and Aggression in Boys Groups: Developmental and Contextual Analyses. *Child Development,61*: 1289–1309.

Ericson, N. (2001). *Addressing the Problem of Juvenile Bullying*. OJJDP Fact Sheet #27. U.S. Department of Justice, Office of Justice Programs, Office of Juvenile Justice and Delinquency Prevention. Washington, DC: U.S. Government Printing Office.

Elliott, D.S. (1994). *Youth Violence: An Overview*. Boulder, CO: University of Colorado, Center for the Study and Prevention of Violence.

Farrington, D.P. (1993). Understanding and Preventing Bullying. In M. Tonry and N. Morris (Eds). *Crime and Justice*, Vol. 17. Chicago: University of Chicago Press.

Hawkins, D.L., Pepler, D.J., and Craig, W.M. (2001). Naturalistic Observations of Peer Interventions in Bullying. *Social Development, 19*: 512-527.

Haynie, D.L., Nansel, T.R., Eitel, P., Crump, A.D., Saylor, K., Yu, K.,and Simons-Morton, B. (2001). Bullies, Victims, and Bully/Victims: Distinct Groups of At-Risk Youth. *Journal of Early Adolescence, 21*: 29–49.

Lawrence R. (1998). *School Crime and Juvenile Justice*. New York: Oxford University Press.

Loeber, R., and Stouthamer-Loeber, M. (1998). Juvenile Aggression at Home and at School. In Elliott, D.S., Hamburg, B.A., and Williams, K.R. (Eds.), *Violence in American Schools: A New Perspective* (pp. 94–126). New York, NY: Cambridge University Press.

Nansel, T., Overpeck, M., Pilla, R., Ruan, J., Simons-Morton, B., and Scheidt, P. (2001). Bullying Behaviors Among U.S. Youth: Prevalence and Association With Psychosocial Adjustment. *Journal of the American Medical Association, 285*: 2094–2100.

Nansel, T., Overpeck, M., Haynie, D., Ruan, J. and Scheidt, P. (2003). Relationships Between Bullying and Violence Among US Youth. *Archives of Pediatric and Adolescent Medicine, 157*: 348–353.

Olweus, D. (1999). Bullying in Sweden. In Smith, P.K., Morita, Y., Junger-Tas, J. Olweus, D., Catalanao, R., and Slee, P. (Eds). *The Nature of School Bullying: A Cross-National Perspective*. New York: Routledge.

Olweus, D. (1997). Bully/Victim Problems in School: Knowledge Base and an Effective Intervention Program. *The Irish Journal of Psychology, 18*: 170–190.

Olweus, D. (1993) *Bullying at School: What We Know and What We Can Do*. Cambridge, MA: Blackwell.

Olweus, D., (1991). Bully/Victim Problems Among School Children: Some Basic Facts and Effects of a School-based Intervention Program. In Pepler, D. and Rubin, K. (Eds.) *The Development and Treatment of Childhood Aggression*, (pp. 411–438). Hillsdale, NJ: Earlbaum.

Olweus, D. (1980). Familial and Temperamental Determinants of Aggressive Behavior in Adolescent Boys: A Causal Analysis. *Developmental Psychology, 16*: 644–660.

Olweus, D. (1978). Aggression in the Schools. Bullies and Whipping Boys. Washington, DC: Hemisphere Press (Wiley).

Pellegrini, A., and Bartini, M. (2001). Dominance in Early Adolescent Boys: Affiliative and Aggressive Dimensions and Possible Functions. *Merrill-Palmer Quarterly, 47*: 142–63.

Pellegrini, A., and Long, J. (2002). A Longitudinal Study of Bullying, Dominance, and Victimization During the Transition from Primary School Through Secondary School. *British Journal of Developmental Psychology, 20*, 259–280.

Smith, P., Dowie, H., Olafsson, R., and Liefooghe, A. (2002). Definitions of Bullying: A Comparison of Terms Used, and Age and Gender Differences, in a Fourteen-Country International Comparison. *Child Development, 73*: 1119–1133.

Underwood, M.K., Galen, B.R., and Paquette, J.A. (2001). Top Ten Challenges for Understanding Gender and Aggression in Children: Why Can't We All Just Get Along? *Social Development, 10*: 248-266.

Wilton, M.M., Craig, W., and Pepler, D. (2000). Emotional Regulation and Display in Classroom Victims of Bullying: Characteristic Expressions of Affect, Coping Styles and Relevant Contextual Factors. *Social Development, 9*: 226–245.

D

E

F

INDEX

A

B

C

G

H

I

J

L

M

S

T

U

V

W

Y

Healthcare Happily Ever After

A Friendly Little Tale of the Health Savings Account and How It Won the Heart of a Nation

Robert Hopper, Ph.D., and Debra Hopper

Published by:
A.D. Banker & Company®, L.L.C.
5000 College Blvd. #120
Overland Park, KS 66211
www.adbanker.com
1-800-866-2468

International Standard Book Number (ISBN)
ISBN 978-0-9773986-1-4

Printed in the U.S.A.

This book provides an overview of how the health savings account functions. Because the health savings account has tax implications, it is advisable to consult with a tax advisor before making financial decisions based upon tax benefits. No representations are made as to the materials completeness or accuracy, although A.D. Banker & Company®, L.L.C has made every effort to confirm facts about HSAs in this book prior to publication. The views expressed in this book are the views of the authors and do not necessarily reflect the views of A.D. Banker & Company®, L.L.C. or its affiliates or subsidiaries.

This is a fiction book. Names, characters, places, and events either are the product of the authors' imagination or are used fictitiously, and any resemblance to real people, living or dead, is entirely coincidental.

This book is not intended for young children and may or may not be appropriate for young children. Whether it is or is not appropriate is left to the discretion of parents/guardians.

FOREWORD

16 November 2006

To the average American, the healthcare system seems more than a little confusing. In a country where we are fortunate to have access to the finest healthcare in the world, without waiting lists, without rationing, and without the heavy hand of government interfering in our choices, the ability to afford the cost of such a premier system can seem overwhelming. Although employers have fortunately supported this system with both their time and money in the past, rising costs are dictating that changes must be made.

As we all know, change can be both frightening and a blessing. It is human nature that we often cling to what is familiar, even if it doesn't serve our long-term interests. Although many of the potential remedies to today's rising costs represent an exciting opportunity for consumers, understanding the new options and opportunities can be daunting. Employers, agents and brokers and others who are charged with explaining the options and how to use them in the best possible way are often challenged with how to do so in a simple and easy-to-understand manner. This book takes much of the mystery out of that equation. In short, its fresh look could change forever the way you feel about healthcare in America.

Bob and Debra Hopper's newest work provides an entertaining look at healthcare and provides some solutions in a way that every American will enjoy reading. It addresses problems with our healthcare system and presents consumer-directed healthcare as a possible solution not just for the healthy and wealthy, but for everyone. The story format presents a message that is frankly not getting out via other means. The authors present a hybrid approach to Democratic and Republican healthcare policy and bravely venture their thoughts on other important policy issues. Be prepared for a new way of looking at healthcare—it's time well spent on an issue of vital national importance.

Janet Trautwein

Executive Vice President and CEO

The National Association of Health Underwriters

Healthcare Happily Ever After

A Friendly Little Tale of the Health Savings Account and How It Won the Heart of a Nation

On a rain-soaked night in Washington, D.C., a young man tightens his trench coat against the pelting summer rain and pauses beneath a streetlamp to make sure he hasn't been followed. He darts down a dark alleyway and silently climbs a staircase. A door swings open easily, exposing him to the raucous clatter of a restaurant kitchen—saucepans scraping, plates rattling in the hands of waiters, and the bellow of the tyrannical chef to get him out of there.

Shrugging his collar to conceal his identity, he trips backwards into a warm restaurant vibrating with clear soft light and the press of a Saturday night crowd of diners. Raindrops glide off his coat and puddle at his feet.

There…across the room. He spies the familiar sunny face of his parents' most trusted friend and makes his way stealthily to the corner table, but the individual sees him and raises a hand to wave. Matt cringes, his cover blown. He leans across the table and whispers, "You told me this was a secret meeting."

"No, Matt, I said to be *discreet*. And what were you doing in the kitchen?"

Matt shrugs sheepishly and attempts an explanation. "…I was pursuing a primal male instinct for intrigue?"

His companion chuckles fondly. "Take a seat, Matt, and find a safe place for your decoder ring."

Matt sits, happy to be here on this rainy night with his mentor. Though separated in age by almost four decades, the unlikely pair shares a love of politics. In the inner circles of the great political grid of the Beltway, Matt is aide to this seasoned legislator who leans back easily and says, "I suppose you are wondering why I asked you here?"

They laugh at the old line. Matt holds up a hand. "Allow me. You've finally decided to put yourself in the running for the presidential election."

His colleague grins. "You certainly know how to steal my thunder."

Matt raises his glass in a toast. "To you. America is waiting." Silently, he thinks, *Thank you, thank you, thank you.* Across the table sits the person he respects above all others, moderate yet courageous enough to stand firm against both union leaders and CEOs, fearless in espousing the politically incorrect, farseeing, steely, flexible and wise and possessed of a sparkling wit.

The future candidate raises an eyebrow. "Permission to interrupt your private thoughts?"

Matt smiles. "Caught me cataloging your virtues." He takes a bite of salad.

"Why, thank you. While you catalog, ponder this, my energetic, political wunderkind. Considering all potential foreign and domestic issues, do you still believe as I do that healthcare will decide the next president?"

"Yep—hm, good cucumbers—healthcare remains the number one domestic issue in America. We spend more per capita than anywhere in the world, but one in six Americans doesn't have protection." Matt stares at his baked potato, then lavishes it first with butter and then with sour cream. "The system's dysfunctional, what can I say?"

His mentor adds, "Yes, and insurance premiums continue to skyrocket, ballooning at three times the rate of normal inflation—are you really going to eat that?"

Matt rolls his eyes. "Mhm, oh, it's so good this way—and yes, people are worn out. If you ask me, they're ready for a miracle."

"It might take one. When aging baby boomers lean their full weight on the system, their healthcare expenses alone will surpass the entire Federal budget."

"Scary. I don't know…seems to me, as a nation, we're more unhealthy than we used to be." Matt takes another bite of the larded potato.

His mentor watches. "Yes…an open door for diabetes, heart disease and cancer."

They sit quietly, recalling the many attempts to wrestle this problem to the ground. Matt touches his napkin to his mouth. "You know you're the one to do this, don't you? You really are the one."

"And you know I will not stop at victory. I mean to see America united."

"Find a brand-new, earth-shattering strategy to excite both Democrats and Republicans, and you will be President, I guarantee."

"As Einstein said, 'You cannot solve problems with the same level of thinking that created the problem in the first place.'" Without warning, the presidential hopeful plops a thick binder onto the table. *Thunk!*

Matt stares at it. "What's this?"

"All the data—five pounds and three solid inches summarizing the great healthcare debates: Universal Coverage, the Canadian system, Single Payer, Free Enterprise, Consumer-Directed…including a mountain of political and journalistic response. A full Internet search—and some unpublished sources."

Matt is confused. "So…you've already found the solution?"

The presidential hopeful looks frustrated. "There are so many choices; I sometimes shake my head. I look at the Single-Payer model, with government paying for everything, and I have this fear: If I remodeled my house and didn't like the results, I could try again. But if I leveled the property, the house would be lost forever. Once we switch to total government control, if it doesn't work, how will we reverse the damage? First I'd like to entertain every possibility of fixing our current system—if at all possible. Insurance companies need to play a part, government must meet its responsibilities, citizens need to pitch in and healthcare providers will play a role, but how?"

"Right. How?"

"And this is where you come in, young sprout. I am enlisting your help—not that of my aging cronies—because you are the future. Healthcare will either make or break your generation so you need to have a say."

"—And because you wouldn't dare choose anyone else." Matt finishes his Key lime pie and grins. "This may surprise you, but I enjoy a wide sphere of influence."

They laugh.

"Seriously," Matt continues, "all it takes is talking to enough people—those who share our concerns, who also remember how to speak the truth—"

"Though it may not be politically correct—or in their best financial interests?"

Matt reaches for his trench coat. "Exactly. I'm on it...*Prez*."

CHAPTER ONE

THE CAUSE OF RISING PREMIUMS

Thunk. Thunk. ...Thunk.

Morgan le Fay, CEO of Middle Road Think Tank, circles a conference table and drops a thick binder in front of three seated economists. Familiar with the dramatic urgencies of their formidable boss, the three economists are variously bored and nervous. They await the punch line cautiously. At six feet tall, Morgan easily oversees the operations of this nonpartisan think tank. She also wants everything now.

Her low, sultry voice is like a velvet hammer. "Good afternoon. What a fine Friday."

Keith Longview sinks down in his seat as visions of his golf weekend go up in smoke. At forty-five, he is the oldest member of this small organization.

Stephanie, twenty-seven and a graduate, summa cum laude, of Harvard, says in a bored voice, "I hear the tolling of midnight hours."

"Yes," replies Morgan, delightedly, "don't you just love Friday afternoon emergency meetings?" She flips to page one of the three-inch thick binder. Her three economists do the same. Keith reads the opening line...

REQUEST: Determine the Cause of Skyrocketing Insurance Premiums

...and groans, now convinced his golf clubs will never leave the bag—not this weekend.

Eunice, the third member of the team, seems confused. Stephanie raises a willowy arm. Her suit is an original Dior, purchased in Paris. "Pleeeze, I get so tired of the healthcare wars. Let everyone pay their own way. Why all the fuss?"

"Oh, right," says Eunice jumping in, "easy for you to say, with that trust fund of yours—why do you even work?"

"Because Daddy says I need to use my *big, gorgeous brain*."

Eunice makes a face at Stephanie. "Your brain isn't any bigger than mine."

"Now, now, children," Keith interjects, "let's keep it to a dull roar."

Morgan raises an eyebrow. "Mr. Longview? Care to enlighten us?"

"There is a 'fuss' because healthcare may bankrupt the entire system, destroying my ability to retire someday—which means I'll be enjoying the company of you three enchanting beings until I dry up and die."

Morgan laughs, a moment of glee before the steel returns to her eyes. "Dear colleagues." She hoists the binder and holds it high. "There are reputations to be made, rapid upward mobility. But if we fail, I'm sure you'll find your way to the soup kitchen."

Stephanie rolls her eyes and says in a bored voice, "Why us? We're not specialists in healthcare."

"Stephanie," Morgan purrs, "ever heard the word *politics*? We are preparing a position statement for a probable candidate for the presidency."

The room buzzes.

"—Unlike think tanks funded by either Republican or Democrat, thanks to my substantial fortunes, we don't bark or bite for anybody—not unless I say so."

Keith leans forward. "But—and I'm guessing—we got the contract because we're clueless in the arena of healthcare and thus hold a fresh perspective?"

"Precisely—not to mention my friends in high places. But, getting down to business...because this is a two-party issue, I am splitting you, my team, in two. Stephanie and Eunice, I want the two of you to scour the research and bring me the head of the problem on a platter."

Eunice cringes.

"Keith, wipe your slate clean." Morgan extends one perfectly manicured fingernail and scoots the binder away from him. "I don't want your nose in anybody's research. Ignore all preconceptions about health insurance and find my answer."

"Delightful," deadpans Keith, "just meditate and spill forth my enlightenment?"

Morgan grins ironically. "As long as your spilling forth gives me my answer by eight a.m. Monday." She checks her watch. "It is now five o'clock on Friday. A good sixty-three hours of meditation should lose or save your job."

Back in his office, Keith stares blankly at his wall of books, an idea percolating. Ah, yes, management expert Tom Peters' *In Search of Excellence*, wherein the best executives and managers spent considerable time walking about, talking to employees and customers.

He bounces out of his chair. Maybe the experts in the ivory towers aren't talking to the real folks who pay the premiums. What if he were to survey random citizens, learning what they like and dislike about insurance?

He snatches an invitation from the corner of his desk for an evening fundraiser for a local charity. The timing couldn't be better. Random sampling has always been a good friend of the economist and, tonight, several hundred people will be in attendance, never dreaming they will play an important role in formulating a national healthcare solution.

Two hours later he hands his car keys to the valet and chuckles. *Not a bad place for a little walking about.* The expansive lawn of the hillside estate boasts a dazzling view of the harbor. The Torchlighters, a quintet of local musicians, plays polite jazz while three hundred guests sample hors d'oeuvres from banquet tables lined up like dominoes. At the ocean end of the lawn, a martini bar hosts a congregation of the faithful and Keith moves in for the first interview. He takes a sip of his lemon drop martini and, with a barely audible cough, mumbles the phrase, "health insurance."

Alice, a fluttering blond with diamonds on her fingers, turns and says, "Oh, don't get me started. I hate health insurance."

Keith moves a step closer.

"Don't get me wrong," she purrs, "I luuuuv my health plan, who wouldn't? A $25 copay for prescriptions—do you have any idea how much my medications would cost if I had to pay the full price? Don't ask. Something like four times the amount—and my insurance has a good annual exam benefit, but the plan is not the problem."

"You got that right," says an energetic senior. "Thomas is the name—call me Tom. I'm trying to save for retirement in two years! Why can't those insurance companies figure out the correct premium and just leave it at that?"

Georgia, a dark-eyed beauty steps into their circle. "Mhm. My company used to pay 100% of the premium—everything you could want—but our CEO is throwing increases at us with the option of choosing cheaper plans with inferior benefits."

A young man in blue jeans and a tie-dyed shirt raises his glass. "Greetings. Couldn't help but eavesdrop. Tired of insurance gouging? It's simple. Adopt a national healthcare plan like Canada or Europe—government pays it all."

"Oh, bosh," says Tom. "Quality goes right down the drain—how would you like to stand in line while you wait for a transplant?"

"What's that like?" asks Alice.

"Do we really want to go there?" adds Georgia, taking a sip of her martini and wandering away, muttering, "*Liberals…*"

The debate gains and loses steam, people wander back and forth, and Keith gets an earful. Left alone after an hour, he's crunched their conversations down to a few axioms:

- All in all, folks love low copays for office visits and prescription drugs. As Alice put it so eloquently, they don't want to pay the *real* cost of healthcare.
- Universally, they hate the rising premiums and, as Thomas put it, want insurance companies to fix a stable, unwavering rate.
- Outside the scope of Keith's assignment is the question raised by the lad in the tie-dye and shot down by Tom and Georgia: should we have a government-run system like Canada or Europe?

Mission accomplished, Keith is about to leave when a weary young woman in white shirt and black trousers approaches with a tray of steaming appetizers. She attempts a wan smile and asks, "Care for a crab cake?"

"I'd love one." He accepts the fragrant tidbit and realizes his data is skewed. This fundraiser is for busy society bees with money to spare and the security of owning health insurance. But he hasn't yet polled the opinion of any of the worker bees. "How do you like your health insurance?" he asks offhandedly.

"Me?" The young woman does a double-take. "I don't think you want to talk to me. I'm just here serving the food." The flash of her dark eyes reminds Keith of something…something from his youth.

"Actually, yes—and you're doing a great job. I'm Keith."

"Thanks. I'm Devonne. Sorry I get combative. I'm a single mom—sometimes I feel invisible."

"Understandable."

"Tell the truth, I don't own health insurance—I heard you talking to those other people. My employer doesn't offer it, and no way can I afford the monthly premium for myself—or my little girl. She's eight. At the end of the month I'm lucky if there's money for a movie—I don't have a handful of diamonds like that one lady."

Keith nods his head in the direction of the servers at the banquet table. "What about them? Same story?"

"Far as I know, nobody has insurance. They take their kids to the emergency room, or they go to the clinics. Some of them, when they get sick, they drive overnight to Mexico. They're here legally, in case you're wondering, but they get healthcare over the border for a cost they can afford."

"Doesn't it bother you to work so hard and still not have enough to buy health insurance?"

"You're joking, right? Canada's white and rich—and they can do it. And Mexico is poor and people of color—and they can do it. We should be able to. Do you think I enjoy lying awake at night thinking, 'What if something happens to me? Who's gonna take care of my daughter?' Our government should see what's happening and offer to help the people who really need it—and not by giving them the worst and the lowest."

That night, Keith can't sleep, and it has nothing to do with Morgan's deadline. He can't stop thinking about Devonne and her little girl. To give them credit, Thomas, Alice and Georgia are righteously bugged about rising premiums, but they do not face imminent financial catastrophe if something goes wrong. Clearly, rising premiums are shutting out the Devonnes of America.

He glances at the clock and groans. Three a.m. Early mornings have always been his creative hours—just not *this* early. He stumbles out of bed and fixes a double espresso. His faithful hound, Hugo, stretches into an intricate yoga posture then follows his master lazily. Settling down at his desk, Keith takes a scalding sip of coffee to clear his head as Hugo curls up at his feet and returns to sleep.

As an economist, Keith is fond of simple, basic models. He loves a fresh sheet of paper, a sharp pencil and the challenge of articulating a problem and presenting its solution.

He thinks back to how it used to work, back when he was six and contracted double pneumonia and had to go to the hospital. Because his parents did not have sufficient savings to pay for hospital expenses, they held an insurance policy, the old-fashioned kind—no copays, no prescription drug coverage, no dental, no vision. No rice, no beans, just the enchilada, which meant hospital care only.

For health, car, or home insurance, it was all the same. Keith's mom and dad joined many other people in paying a monthly premium, transferring the risk of financial devastation to an insurance company.

In the case of health insurance, the insurance company pooled the premiums paid by all the moms and dads and, when necessary—as when Keith was rushed to the hospital—paid the hospital directly. Thus the term *third-party payment*.

Since only a few needed to go to the hospital, the pool of money was guaranteed to stay liquid. The insurance company paid all expenses except for the deductible.

First Party	Hospital
Second Party	Keith's parents
Third Party	Insurance Company (the guarantor against devastating expenses)

The three-party transaction works well for insurable events, those big expenses that catch people by surprise.

Keith drops his pencil and gropes around on the floor. The pencil surfaces attached to a dust bunny, and his dog Hugo wakes and whines. "Later, big guy. Daddy will walk you later." *Where was I? Oh, yes...the insurable event, like when my house burns down, my car is totaled or I have a $65,000 hospital bill.*

To illustrate, Keith decides to stay with the analogy of home insurance—not murky and volatile like health insurance. For the concept of insurance to work, a large group of people must be willing to pay a small monthly premium to an insurance company in exchange for the insurance company paying large costs for the few people with claims. In actuality the consumer is saying, "Yikes! I wouldn't be able to handle it if my house burned down." And the insurance company says, "Okay, I'll assume that risk for all of you. If you each give me a little money (in the form of a premium), when disaster strikes there'll be some cash to help out the unlucky few." Keith tracks the money:

Small Premium → Insurance Company → Claims of a Few

He reflects. *It's a numbers game and, come to think of it, a very humanistic system: the many, caring for the needy few.* He refills his espresso cup and wonders what the world would be like without java. "Here, Hugo, come onto the porch."

Keith stands on the back porch in his bathrobe. It is five a.m. He stares at the horizon, where one line of golden light promises a new day, and realizes he is not just compiling a report for his boss. In this gift of hours, he is actually in dialogue with a future President of the United States, sharing his best ideas for the care of the health of America. He can readily prepare something that skates along the surface, something to appease Morgan and look good on the page. Or he can invest himself in the endeavor and thereby become a piece of history.

He inhales the sweet fragrance of the dawn breeze, and suddenly his thoughts are circling around Devonne, the server at last night's fundraiser. He can't chase her out of his mind. Those wide, calm eyes and that weary smile; the hard, grinding job of scratching together enough money. A memory is triggered, rolling back the years…

…He'd been such a teenaged fool, but the feelings of love had been true. Chauncey was her name, a girl hardworking and devoted to her family, like Devonne. *What had gone wrong?* Keith flinches. His mother had been a beast about it, something about not wanting him to mingle with girls from the other side of the tracks. It all seemed so harsh and so long ago…

He runs a hand through his hair. *What's all this foolishness? Must be the lack of sleep. I'm a scientist, maybe even a philosopher, but a romantic?*

Keith shakes his head to clear it. It is his job to engineer a cold, calculating system of economics, nothing more. Hugo barks, interrupting his reverie. "Back inside. Daddy has a report to write." *Where was I? Oh, yes...the gist of insurance.*

It seems to him the insurance concept works for three reasons.

1. Claims are too large to save for. It is difficult enough to afford a mortgage, let alone save sufficient money to rebuild a home in case of fire. Insurance is a much better solution.
2. Claims are unexpected and could happen to anyone. It is a random and devastating event for a house to burn down.
3. People are willing to pay the small premium on the off-chance they'll need the big protection. A $500 annual premium is a wise investment against rebuilding a $300,000 home destroyed by fire.

Keith makes a third cup of espresso, stands up to stretch and opens the shades. He squints at the bright morning sunlight. Hugo whines and scratches at the door. Keith ignores him for two minutes before a howl to shake the house down inspires him to action. "Okay, big guy. You're right."

They set out on their walk, Hugo snuffling at every other shrub and Keith thinking back to 35 years ago, when his mom used to take him to the doctor. His mother had insisted on graciousness and beauty in all things—doctor's offices included.

He smiles, recalling the office filled with framed paintings and ornate vases of flowers. The doctor was friendly, and five-year-old Keith was in love with the pretty nurse—something his proper mother would never have approved.

In the old days, when insurance premiums were not skyrocketing, the doctor, or first party, provided a service, usually a check-up and a tetanus booster, which Keith hated. Keith's mom, the second party, paid at the time of service—cash on the spot. Likewise, when his mom stopped at the pharmacy, she paid the bill—again, cash on the spot.

This is the center of it, Keith tells himself, jotting down a quick note. *This is where everything changed and we lost control of our economic balance.* "Hugo," he calls out, "let's put some spring in our step." Man and dog break into a run.

After a healthy shower and a bite to eat, a refreshed Keith Longview is ready to dive back in. Hugo is happy with his new squeaky toy, and Keith is thinking how different things are from when he was a boy. Back then, third-party payment took care of the big, unexpected expenses, like his visit to the hospital. On the other hand, his mom and dad paid the routine anticipated expenses, like the yearly visits to see the pretty nurse. *But today,* Keith thinks, *people expect insurance to pay what Mom and Dad used to pay, cash on the spot...*

A light bulb goes off in his head. *This is what makes insurance too expensive! People expect insurance to take care of everything! Is this good? Is it bad?*

Is it working? No. Insurance was originally designed to cover insurable events, not to be used for every cough and sputter and ache. Insurance is meant to be the friend who's "got your back," as they say in the movies; not the parent who pays all your expenses. Keith draws a table contrasting different types of insurance.

	Small, Routine and Expected	Large but Expected	Large and Unexpected
Auto	Lube job	Upgrade from Saturn to BMW roadster	Car totaled in head-on collision
Home	Repair a window latch	Remodel a kitchen	Rebuild the garage after a fire
Health	Office visit for a cold	Maternity expenses	Hugely expensive care for infant born prematurely

Keith knows that historically insurance was never meant to be a maintenance agreement, but to cover large unexpected events. This is the only way it works and the only way to keep premiums affordable. To deviate in any way always gives a result of rising premiums.

Maintenance is not an insurable event. Standard maintenance for a car is not insurable. People don't expect automobile insurance to pay for oil changes or a new set of tires or engine repairs. Likewise, standard maintenance for the care of a home is not insurable. People don't expect home insurance to paint the house or upgrade the old kitchen with a remodel. These are the expected costs of owning a car or a home.

Any deviation from classic insurance causes a rise in premiums. Standard maintenance for the care of a body—like it or not—does not fall under the classic definition of an insurable event. People should not expect health insurance to pay the routine costs of daily living. An office visit to a doctor is a simple cost of living, like food and clothing. No one wanders in a blizzard naked or goes two weeks without food just because insurance doesn't cover food and clothing. Why do they expect insurance to pay for all the routine, expected expenses of healthcare? And what happens when insurance companies *do* pay these costs? *Bingo!* Keith scribbles a note.

The Cause of Rising Premiums

Hallelujah! In the territory of pure economics, Keith leaves pencil and paper and jumpstarts the computer. Morgan did not hire him to question whether the system was wrong or right but merely to find the *economic* truth of the matter. He opens a new document and begins typing.

Third-party payment of non-insurable events is the cause of rising premiums.

When insurance companies (Third Party) pay a portion of non-insurable events (copays for office visits, prescriptions, labs and X-rays), this distorts our system of economics—preventing the free marketplace from controlling prices at their proper level.

Keith smiles and mutters to himself, "In sophisticated terms, it screws things up." Checking the printer to make sure he has paper, he types the major points to support his thesis…

- **Copays—friend or foe?**
  - Copays mask the real costs of healthcare. A $20 copay masks the real cost of a $65 office visit to a general practitioner or a $100 charge for a specialist.
  - They put medical services ON SALE. A prescription drug costs $100 but the consumer pays only $25, a 75% discount. Someone must make up the difference to the drug company.
  - They prevent price competition between providers. Logically, the most experienced doctor should get paid more than a fledgling physician just out of medical school. But if all doctor visits are $20, copays prevent this from happening. There is no price competition. The backlash is that many of the best doctors prefer not to be on insurance company preferred networks, with more of them either leaving networks every year or leaving the practice of medicine entirely. In any system—free market or otherwise—experience and expertise have to count for something.
- **Low deductibles put medium-priced services ON SALE.** Taking advantage of a low deductible and a coinsurance benefit of 20%, the consumer pays $700 for a $1,500 MRI. That's a 50% discount, and someone must make up the difference to the MRI lab.

- **Sale prices cause a catastrophic chain reaction.**
  - o Sale prices modify behavior and dramatically increase the use of healthcare services. When someone catches a cold or flu, the best treatment might be to go to bed, take two aspirin, drink plenty of fluids, and rest. But with an affordable $20 copay, why not see the very best doctor in town, request lab tests and demand a prescription or two?
  - o Increased claims lead to increased premiums. While the insured only pays the copay, the insurance company is still on the hook, required to pay the remainder of the provider's fees, using premiums to pay those claims. With more claims to pay, they are forced to increase premiums.
  - o As premiums rise, consumers try to get the most benefit. Instead of striving to be frugal in the use of health insurance and to make every effort to keep ourselves abundantly healthy, we try to milk our plans for every last benefit—whether necessary or not. We don't do this with home insurance or car insurance. When we get a small dent in our car, we avoid making an insurance claim because we know a premium increase will follow.

Keith stops typing and reviews. *That's the problem in a nutshell. Now what to do about it.*

- **Remove the ON SALE features of health plans to control rising premiums.** Unless the get-more-for-less mentality is removed, consumers will continue to stream in the door, using healthcare services they may not need and do not know the cost of.

  A retail store that keeps its merchandise forever ON SALE will quickly go out of business. This is a law in the world of free market enterprise, the economics of capitalism. To do it any other way means shifting to another economic basis; socialism, for example. But in the free market system, in order to avoid the specter of going out of business, health insurance companies raise premiums and therefore keep their doors open, insuring Americans against large, unexpected expenses.

Alone at his desk, Keith beams. The afternoon is not yet gone… looks like the chance of golf might still be on the horizon. Two final points, a masterful summary and then the first tee.

- o Allow insurance companies to do what they do best—provide affordable coverage for insurable events only.

  This translates into a simple, high-deductible health plan, with consumers paying all costs up to the deductible and insurance companies paying costs after the deductible—just as our parents used to do and exactly as is done with home insurance and car insurance. Unburdened by the necessity of paying claims below the deductible amount, insurance companies could charge substantially less for their plans. Competition among insurance companies for new policyholders would keep premiums low.

- o Allow consumers to do what they do best—use their own dollars to shop for the best values in healthcare.

  Consumers would voice their approval by shopping around for the best combination of quality, service and price. By saving money each month on premiums, the wise consumer could open a savings account and thereby save for future, routine, and expected healthcare expenses as well as build a nest egg to pay for future insurance deductibles.

Keith goes to the top of the document and types *Executive Summary*. He doesn't look back as he grabs his golf bag and car keys and heads out the door.

Monday morning bright and early, Keith, Stephanie and Eunice face Morgan le Fay across the conference table. She holds two separate reports—one, thick and elegantly bound; the other, a single page, unbound. As always, she stands for dramatic effect.

"Alright…if I am lucky, and if *you* are lucky, I have in my hands the best of your bright minds. Keith, you relied on real life experience—I'm so pleased you had such a productive time at the fundraiser

Friday night"—she waves the single page of paper constituting his entire report.

"Eunice, Stephanie, just thumbing through your extensive *tome*, it looks as if all three of you are in rhythm. Insurance for the big stuff, and consumers pay the small bills. Time will reveal if our client is as satisfied as I am with your results."

Morgan graces them all with her sly smile. "Stand up and congratulate yourselves…I'll march you all to the restaurant of your choice—dinner on me tonight," she laughs, "—as soon as we prepare a dazzling presentation for our client."

Eunice and Stephanie file out of the room. Morgan turns at the door. "Mr. Longview? Not coming?"

"In a minute," he says. He waits until Morgan closes the door, then sits for a quiet moment, meditating on the past. Eventually his thoughts catch up to the present, but he cannot wipe the memory of Devonne from his mind.

He's prepared an excellent report, professional to the last degree, entitled, "Third-Party Payment of Small Medical Bills Is the Cause of Skyrocketing Premiums."

He stares out the window. He has failed to fully enter into a dialogue with the future. A precious thread is left hanging. *Devonne is one of millions, hardworking but always poor. Just because she cannot afford to go to Harvard, she should not be denied the prosperity of America.* Keith circles his pencil on a blank page. *Something must be done for Devonne and her daughter, for the poor of America.*

* * * * * * *

Matt places a quick call to the unlisted number. When he hears the presidential hopeful at the end of the line, he says, "Just checking in. We're making progress. So far I think everyone agrees that the problem with healthcare is simple—it costs money."

"Oh dear."

"Right?" Matt stares down the street to make sure his car is not being ticketed. "And up to now everyone agrees it is costing too much money—with some experts wanting to place the blame with consumers and some placing it entirely in the laps of the insurance companies and their thirst for profits."

"Well, I suppose the philosophical response to that would be, 'Should something as dear as the health of a nation be a matter of dollars and cents?'"

"Yes, you could go there," agrees Matt, "though a question like that could shake the foundations of our economic system."

"But this is the core issue underlying all argument, 'Should healthcare be free? Or should it cost money? If so, how much—and who should pay for it?'"

"Right, and if it's free, you're living on Mars," says Matt with feeling. "There's no such thing as a free lunch. Someone ultimately pays; either the patient pays for everything, which gives you pure, unrestrained capitalism, or the government pays, which gives you socialized medicine and a tax structure that goes through the roof."

"Don't shoot it down out of hand. Total government funding of healthcare is intuitively pleasing and has a large number of proponents. It appears to be a very compassionate way to go."

"Compassionate?"

"Ideally, everyone is guaranteed affordable access to unlimited healthcare. There's much to be admired. Still, I have my reservations. My research is focused on Canada, which does a great job of routine healthcare—doctor visits and the like; medical services are essentially free. My problem comes with more serious medical problems such as heart disease, cancer, stroke and chronic need for ongoing treatment, technology, surgery and hospital care. If all healthcare, including expensive high-tech treatments, were free and available to everyone and if everyone took advantage of the costly care, the government would go broke. Canada controls costs by limiting the number of specialists such as orthopedic surgeons, cardiologists and oncologists. Also, they limit technology such as MRIs, CT scans, equipment for angiograms and microsurgery."

"Doesn't sound good."

"No. Per capita, compared to Canada, the U.S. has three times the MRI equipment, twice the CT scanners and a hundred times the PET scanners. In Canada's single payer system, if I experience mild chest pain, a primary care physician refers me to a specialist, involving a lengthy wait. Due to limited technology, I wait again for diagnostic testing; and because of limited specialists, another wait for surgical treatment."

"Actually?" interjects Matt, "it sounds like a poorly managed HMO: long waits, lost records, limited access. Scary. Is this why our hospitals and clinics in New York, Boston, Philly, Houston and Miami are filled with Canadians?"

"Could be they're running away from the rationing. In Canada, if I'm 65 and need heart surgery, and you're 25 and need the same thing, I get bumped. At your age I know this doesn't seem threatening, but many Americans are over 55, with all the health problems an aging body encounters."

Matt exhales audibly. "'America: the Ration Nation'—I don't know…I don't like the sound of it. Say, I have a bright idea. How about surgeons, internists, gynecologists and cardiologists offering their services free?"

The legislator laughs uproariously. "Oh, in your dreams, but I do admire your sense of humor."

Matt checks his watch. "Gotta run. Gotta flight to catch. I'll keep in touch."

"Keep in touch with America, Matt. That's all I ask."

CHAPTER TWO

Ideal Health Insurance

About a hundred yards off the California coast, Mary Sumner floats on a vintage ten-foot Velzey Jacobs surfboard. Her sixteen-year-old son, Jordan, floats a few yards behind her. Last night a swell rolled in from Alaska, and they lie in wait for the perfect wave.

Mary would never let Jordan see her tears of appreciation as she stares out to sea. It is a miracle to be here with him, so tall and strong, such a friendly, freckled boy. Sixteen years ago, he fought for life in a hospital incubator, a victim of congenital heart complications. Mary and her husband did not know from day to day if they would be childless, never knowing their struggle would continue through three years of continual operations, their brave son enduring the worst.

What would have happened if there had been no insurance to cover nearly a million dollars in medical bills? Would they have lost Jordan?

No. She erases the thought. He's right here, in the water alongside her…

Her mind jolts to attention as she senses the shoulder of ocean rising up; her strong arms begin paddling, deep and rhythmically. After thirty years of this, she has just enough power to turn her board before the exhilarating elevator lift of the wave. She drops in, trims the board and zooms along the wave's face. Showing off, she dances to the front of the board and hangs five. Peeling into a tube, the wave envelopes her and she re-emerges to the sound of, "Mom!"

Her heart leaps. She drops out of the way as her laughing youngster flies across the crest of a monster wave. In the sunlight, he seems part of the ocean, all sparkling and fresh and full of promise. *Jordan.* Every battle was worth it.

The president of Blue Sky Insurance drops a three-inch, five-pound binder on Mary's desk. *Thunk.* She takes a sip of water and says, "Morning, Howard. What's up?"

Howard closes the door. He *never* closes the door.

"Mary, I've come to talk to you."

"Why did my stomach just tighten into a knot?"

Howard sits in the chair for guests to the office. "I've been asked to do something uncomfortable and confidential, and I need to enlist your help."

"I think this is where I sneak out."

He attempts a chuckle. "You're not going anywhere."

"Okay, then, can we open my door?"

"No, this is confidential. I got a call from a, um, a friend—well, actually, the son of a friend of a friend—he's young but he's a regular whiz kid, and he's stumping around for this friend of a friend, getting the ball rolling for the—"

"Howard?"

Howard blinks.

"Focus, Howard. You already said it's uncomfortable, so let's get it over with."

He frowns. "Ah, yes." He clears his throat. "It's just this: I've been asked to come up with The Ideal Insurance Plan For America—all in capital letters, I assure you. Mary, this is national. This is…political. We need to design a…a master plan, if you will, to truly benefit all Americans—I'm not joking, *really* not joking."

"Whew," says Mary, "for a minute there you had me nervous."

Howard laughs gratefully, then sighs.

Mary's specialty, as Howard's trusted senior vice president in charge of new product development, is small businesses with two to fifty employees. Hired out of college, she has seen the evolution of health insurance from basic hospital coverage to the present indemnity plans, PPOs, HMOs, POSs, EPOs, no-deductible copay plans, and now the HSA-qualified high-deductible health plans. Plans, plans and more plans.

She grins at her boss and says, "Howard, I get it. Now get out of here so I can get to work."

He laughs and leaves.

Finally. Mary stares at the open door, hiding her secret thoughts. She already knows the solution to the healthcare crisis. Replace all insurance products—PPOs, HMOs, POSs—with a simple high-deductible health plan to pay for larger expenses, and insist that consumers open a Health Savings Account to pay for everything else—an idea so scandalous it could cost her job. Shareholders would want her head. It would surely carve a hole in the Blue Sky workforce, with far fewer insurance claims to administer. But to repair America's dysfunctional healthcare system, someone needs to step forward and speak the truth.

She sits rigidly in her chair, not exactly ready to lose her job. If she lived in a perfect world, what would she really want from an insurance plan? *Easy,* she muses... *everything...* and I'd want it to be *free.* Or very close to it. Tired from her encounter with Howard, she closes her eyes and drifts into a light sleep.

Whoosh! She is encircled in golden light as a magical being in white robes floats down into the chair recently vacated by Howard and a mellifluous, otherworldly voice says, "For the rest of your life, you will spend less than $500 per year on healthcare."

In her sleep, Mary thinks, *If I knew I would never spend more than $500 in any calendar year, I would never buy insurance again.* The air hums with celestial harmonies and *Whoosh!* The mystical being appears a notch less confident. "Oops, there's been a slight change. Did I mention that at some point in the next ten years you'll have a major illness with surgery and hospitalization? I'm not sure when, but don't worry, you'll will recover quickly, and it won't be painful, except for the shock of medical bills exceeding $250,000. *Whoosh!*

Mary awakens, a bit unsettled, realizing she would definitely purchase insurance against the unexpected large claim now looming in her hypothetical future. She gets on the phone to Egbert, the chief actuary on the fourth floor. "Bertie, can you drop what you're doing and take an elevator ride? Need to pick your brain."

It takes only five minutes. Egbert is organized, thorough, responsible and meticulous. He also has the smallest hands and the largest shoes Mary has ever seen on a man. As an actuary, he is the one who looks at populations of people, and varieties and costs of insurance plans, to decide how much the company must charge per plan, in order to stay in business.

"Bertie, from an actuarial standpoint, just exactly how much money does a typical citizen spend on healthcare?"

Egbert, not one to waste words, writes down three numbers and says simply, "Anybody who buys health insurance needs to understand the 68%, 24%, 8% rule."

"Okay," says Mary, "thanks for coming up."

Egbert laughs and launches into his favorite pastime: explaining the mystery behind the numbers. "On average, in America," he instructs Mary, "about 68% of people spend $500 per year on healthcare, and, of those, half spend $0."

"Is that a zero? Do you mean that half of them spend absolutely nothing?"

"Yes, ma'am."

"Two out of three Americans are really that healthy?"

"You betcha. Some experts say 73%—nearly three out of four—Americans spend that little, but just to be safe I stick with 68% spending less than $500 per year."

Mary quickly interjects, "That's me, but I didn't realize I was in the company of so many other healthy people—" but Egbert is on to the next number.

"The 24% represents the number of people who average around $1,000 in healthcare each year. These are people with some form of ongoing expense, usually a prescription drug for cholesterol, allergies, depression, and the like—"

"—and 8%? What is the significance of that number?"

"These policyholders average $12,000 per year. This category takes into account larger medical expenses totaling in the thousands and hundreds of thousands."

"So, there is a one in twelve, or 8%, chance of having a large claim?"

"You got it."

"And the irritating question is, Will this happen to me in year one or year twelve?"

"Yessirree, that's why insurance is one of the greatest and most powerful financial tools ever developed. That is why our company exists today."

"Except, Bertie, both you and I know the healthcare system in this country is going down the tubes."

Egbert makes a face. "I'm an actuary, not a philosopher. If you want opinions, Joni's your gal." He shakes his head, remembering. "She used to be our company's biggest advocate for making health-care affordable and accessible—and pushed us to the brink of giving it all away for free."

"Which would have been a bad thing?"

"Go see Joni."

They order lunch at a sunny outdoor café, and Mary says, "You spearheaded the famous copay plans of the mid-1990s, right? Refresh my memory."

Joni, a senior VP in charge of individual product development, launches in eagerly, loving her work. "*Infamous* is more like it. We thought we had the ideal health plan for America—affordable, accessible, and low in premium. Depending upon your plan you paid a fixed $20, $30 or $40 copay for doctor visits. For outpatient services, we replaced the $500 deductible with a zero deductible. If your doctor recommended a $1,000 fee for labs and X-rays, you simply paid a flat 20% of the cost—two hundred bucks!"

"What about prescription drugs?"

"You only paid a $25 brand-name copay." Disappointment flashes across Joni's face. "Don't get me wrong. Everybody loved these co-pays. Consumers loved them because premiums were so low, there was easy access to physicians, and prescriptions were very affordable. Insurance agents loved the plan because consumers bought them like hotcakes. Insurance companies were ecstatic because they wrote lots of new policies, increasing revenue. Doctors, hospitals and pharmaceutical companies loved them because the insurance company paid most of the bills."

Joni glances down at her taco salad. "I should have been wiser."

"Because...?"

"When everybody likes something, that should be a tip-off that something is wrong. We conducted hundreds of focus groups and built plans based on what consumers told us they wanted. The message was clear: affordable access to routine expected healthcare expenses. In other words: Copays for office visits and copays for prescriptions drugs and no deductibles!"

"But you succeeded in that. You met the consumer demands."

"Yes! And within a year, the poop hit the fan."

Mary hides a smile.

"Insurance companies didn't predict how wildly people would use these plans. Remember? With the old $500 or $1,000 deductible, you stopped and thought before spending money on healthcare. It was your own money; of course you were more careful about how you spent it. But with the new plans, because the insurance company paid a significant portion of every medical bill, it was as if we put healthcare on sale—a 50 to 75 percent discount! People responded like any other sale, crawling over each other to get to the doctor a little more frequently, asking for a few more tests, choosing more expensive prescriptions. It seemed as if overnight every woman you met was on Prozac, because they could get it for a $25 copay instead of the real cost of $100."

Mary shakes her head. "I remember we had to raise premiums after a year—"

"Right, but now we had them addicted to this on-sale mentality. It's as if the insurance companies said to a room full of kids: 'What do you want?' and the kids jumped up and shouted, 'We want chocolate, we want fries, we want cake and we want pies!' The insurance companies gave it to them, and the kids got sick and fat and never learned how to eat right." They weren't about to part with these rich plans, even though the insurance companies were going down the tubes. We *had* to raise the rates!"

"And continued to do so for six years."

"It's been terrible. Our clients got angrier and angrier but—here's the perverse incentive we created—they tried to extract more and more from the plans." Joni pauses and looks truly sad. "The Great Experiment did not work. After six years Blue Sky realized the need for financial restraint—getting rid of the zero deductibles and reinstating deductibles from $500 to $2,500."

"*Jeesh*, I get so emotional, but we tried, Mary, we really did. In the end, we simply got away from our core mission—to provide affordable health insurance protection from large and unexpected medical bills. Our hearts were in the right place, consumers got what they wanted, but it simply did not work. Insurance companies can't pay all the small bills and keep premiums affordable."

Mary nods. "Maybe it's human nature. If the boss is paying for lunch, we order differently than if we're paying for ourselves—unless you're highly disciplined and discerning."

Joni laughs. "Yeah, right. In a perfect world. Golly, I'm the biggest advocate for making healthcare affordable and accessible to all Americans, but I no longer believe copays and low deductibles are the answer."

"You sound like Egbert."

Joni sighs. "Yeah, I guess I've converted."

Mary is thoughtful.

"Here's a chilling statistic," says Joni, looking around and lowering her voice. "On average, in America, employers spend $11,000 per year in premiums for an average family—whether that family has medical expenses or not! Eleven thousand dollars! Just think what you could buy if you were healthy and you had that money in your own pocket!"

Mary is at a loss for words.

"I'm speechless, too," says Joni, getting up from lunch. "It will take better minds than mine to come up with a miraculous solution."

"No, you have a great brain, Joni. Thanks for letting me pick it."

Mary returns to her office and drops out of her shoes, thinking, *Ugh. Can't wear high heels like I used to.* She massages a foot and looks around her office, remembering all the good years she's invested here. It is time to call Howard, but her finger dials Egbert's number instead. "Bertie—can I steal you one more time today?"

"Want me to bring the artillery?"

"What? Oh, oh, sure, bring the artillery."

"Okey-doke. Clear the decks; I'm on my way to the elevator."

Mary glances at her wall clock as she exchanges her high heels for the pair of running shoes she keeps in her bottom drawer. Within five minutes she hears the steady *scrunch-scrunch* of Egbert's enormous shoes coming down the hall. With one pen tucked behind his right ear and another row of pens lined up in his breast pocket, he enters her office carrying a briefcase and an easel. He begins unloading his artillery: a calculator, a file folder, a flip chart and a laptop.

Mary stops him with a question. "Bertie, what do you think is the solution to the healthcare crisis in America?"

Egbert moves to close the door, and Mary cringes. "I didn't like it when Howard tried to do that." Egbert closes the door with finality and turns to face her. "Confidentially, Mary, speaking as a citizen and a friend—not as a professional in the industry—they should clear the decks, and get rid of every superfangled plan and plan permutation, every PPO, HMO, POS—you name it. Send them down the drain. And once the decks are cleared, make high-deductible health plans coupled with Health Savings Accounts available to everyone—no ifs, ands or buts!"

Mary exhales in relief and nods. "How do you propose I present this incendiary idea to Howard?"

Egbert digs in his briefcase and offers her an official one-page Treasury Department Health Savings Account brochure. "It's all outlined here in simple terms. Just hand a copy to Howard the Lion-Hearted and back out of his office very quietly."

"Oh, swell. Thanks, but first I'd like to hear it in your own words."

Bertie's eyes light up. "Okay, let's say you purchase pure major medical insurance—no frills, just the High-deductible health plan with a $3,000 individual deductible. You pay everything *under* $3,000, and the insurance company pays everything *over* $3,000—*always, always,*

always—never varies. It's simple, and it's a bargain. You go to the hospital, you get your open heart surgery, your kidney transplant, your catastrophic burn treatments—insurance pays everything above the $3,000 line."

Egbert stares at Mary pointedly. He knows that sixteen years ago, she faced huge claims with Jordan's lengthy illness. "In our current medical climate," he continues, "nobody does a better job of protecting us from catastrophe than major medical insurance. No one in their right mind should pass it up."

Egbert flips to a clean white page of his flip chart, grabs a marker and illustrates as he talks. "Look…back in the old days, insurance only covered major medical expenses, but now we attach a variety of extras, like a bunch of remora fish attached to the hide of a shark."

"I don't think Howard will appreciate that analogy."

Egbert grins. "I'm gonna make this easy. Think about when you buy a car. The dealer starts with the stripped-down model, a perfectly sound and serviceable automobile. Then, '*for a little extra*' the dealer starts tempting you with the sound system and quickly rachets up the cost with the television in the back '*for the kids*' and then appeals to your need for status in the community by offering '*to the discerning customer*' the luxury exterior, leather seats and pride of ownership. You could save a mountain of money with only standard features, but you purchase more whether you really need it or not. Healthcare is no different."

Egbert grabs a blue marker and quickly sketches a chart. Mary marvels at his small, well-manicured hands. "So," says Egbert, adding a touch of green marker for emphasis, "in your age group, the traditional health plan starts with the major medical plan, and the insurance company attaches the extras:

Traditional Approach: Four Plans in One	
Major medical plan	$180
Office visit plan	$80
Prescription plan	$80
Lab/procedure plan	$60
Monthly totals	$400/mo
Annual totals	$4,800/yr

"I'm going ask you three questions, Mary. Number one. Out of the $400 monthly premium, $80 is apportioned to office visits, whether you go or not. At the end of the year, you've paid $960 for the privilege of forking out a $20 copay. Wouldn't you rather put that money in your pocket?"

"I see the doctor *once* per year and I'm paying $960?"

"Roughly apportioned, yep. Healthy people rarely benefit from having low office visit copay features in their health plan."

"Ouch. What about prescription drugs?"

"Most plans offer a $10 copay for generic drugs, but consumers want the $25 copay for the newest drugs advertised on television." Egbert makes a face. "Boy, is that a racket. Most of the television pills cost a hundred bucks a month—or more. These include ongoing medications for cholesterol, allergies, depression, acid reflux."

"But I don't take any of those."

"Yep, exactly, which leads to question number two. Out of the $400 monthly premium, $80 is apportioned to prescription drugs whether you take them or not. At the end of the year, you've paid $960 for the privilege of purchasing your medications with a $25 copay. Wouldn't you rather put that money in your pocket?"

"And my answer is, *Duh*."

Bertie flinches. "You've been spending too much time with your teenager. Think you can handle question number three? Out of the $400 per month, $60 is apportioned to labs, tests and procedures. At the end of the year, you've paid $720—even if you do not use this feature once. Wouldn't you rather put that money in your pocket?"

"Of course. Every two years I could save enough to pay cash for an MRI or any number of blood tests."

"You and the other 68% to 73% of Americans who are healthy every year just like you. That's why the high-deductible health plan coupled with the health savings account is our good buddy."

Mary is smiling.

"Ready for the finale?" He flourishes a red marker and flips to a clean page.

	Buy HDHP only	Health Savings Account
Major medical plan	$180/mo	
Office visit plan	→	$80/mo or $960/yr
Prescription plan	→	$80/mo or $960/yr
Lab/procedure plan	→	$60/mo or $720/yr
Monthly totals	$180/mo	$220/mo
Annual totals	$2,160/yr	**$2,640/yr**

"Look, you take the $2,640 in saved premiums and put them into a tax-advantaged Health Savings Account. Pay your own routine, expected healthcare, and each year you'll have unused dollars that accrue toward future expenses. The high deductible coupled with the health savings account works supremely well for you."

"Bertie, if I didn't need healthcare for five years, and I haven't for the last five years, I could accumulate over $12,000. If I got really sick, with hospital bills of $100,000 four years in a row, I'd have the cash to meet the annual $3,000 deductible."

"—And, Mary if you call right now, in addition to the pots and pans, you get the six Ginsu cooking knives absolutely free! And you've got yourself a beauty of a healthcare strategy. I have 'em for myself and my wife and kids—wish I could get 'em for the cats and the parrot."

Mary laughs and shakes Egbert's small hand. "Thanks, Bertie. I owe you."

Egbert smiles. "An elegant lunch." He begins to pack up his artillery.

"...*Bertie*?" Mary's voice has shifted in tenor. She realizes, while watching Bertie pack, she has been staring at the framed photo on the far right-hand corner of her desk. Jordan as a three-year-old, previously too sick and too weak to attempt it, but finally taking his first step. A thought keeps nagging her.

"Bertie, what about the uninsured and the uninsurable? What do we do for the working mom who doesn't qualify for Medicaid but doesn't earn enough to buy insurance, not even the high-deductible plan? What happens when she gives birth to her child, only to learn her baby is like Jordan—almost too sick to live? What choices does this mother have? What can the system offer her?"

Egbert considers his words carefully. "Well, I don't know about you, but I have an agreement with my government. I pay my taxes, and I trust them to take care of the needy."

"Bertie, you're full of surprises."

"Shhh," he says, placing a finger to his lips. He leaves with a smile, and Mary drops her eyes to the Treasury's tri-fold brochure, gathering her thoughts for her meeting with Howard the Lion-Hearted by focusing on the pertinent paragraph.

> **High-deductible health plans (HDHPs)**
>
> You must have coverage under an HSA-qualified "high-deductible health plan" (HDHP) to open and contribute to an HSA. Generally, this is health insurance that does not cover first dollar medical expenses. Federal law requires that the health insurance deductible be at least:
>
> $1,100* – self-only coverage
>
> $2,200* – Family coverage
>
> In addition, annual out-of-pocket expenses under the plan (including deductibles, copays and co-insurance) cannot exceed:
>
> $5,500* – self-only coverage
>
> $11,000* – Family coverage
>
> *2007 amounts; adjusted annually for inflation.
>
> In general, the deductible must apply to all medical expense (including prescriptions) covered by the plan. However, plans can pay for "preventive care" services on a first-dollar basis (with or without a co-pay). "Preventive care" can include routine pre-natal and well-child care, child and adult immunizations, annual physicals, mammograms, pap smears, etc.

Today's activities have confirmed Mary's suspicions that, for a large majority, the HDHP coupled with an HSA is the very best plan. But, because the plans require less paperwork, some Blue Sky employees might be out of a job. Because premium revenues will drop for Blue Sky, the shareholders will bellyache. By empowering consumers with HSA dollars and the choice to go where they feel they get the best value, doctors and hospitals will face real price competition.

Pharmaceutical companies will find consumers no longer willing to try out every new drug, like chocolate in a free candy store.

Mary clutches her hands. *And those who cannot afford a deductible are still going to fall through the cracks.* She brightens. Tomorrow will be a new day, and without a doubt, the dawn of change is soon to shake the entire country.

* * * * * * *

Matt flips his cell phone and ducks into the shady doorway of a local hotel to dial the unlisted number. Across the street is the expanse of the Pacific Ocean. When his esteemed colleague, the presidential hopeful, comes on the line, Matt asks, "Ever heard of something called HSA?"

On the other end of the line, the seasoned politician interrupts the onslaught of paperwork to respond. "Sure, the consumer-directed health plans?"

Matt watches an SUV whiz past with four surfboards strapped to the luggage rack. "Is that what they call them up on the Hill? Out here on the left coast they're calling them high-deductible health plans coupled with the Health Savings Account."

"That's eloquent."

"Right," says Matt, nodding. "Someone needs to work on the name."

"Agreed, but called by any name, the consumer-directed health plans line up with a free-market approach to healthcare."

"Great. So you have your healthcare solution."

"No, Matt. Not everyone agrees with a free-market approach. My end goal is to create a unified America."

An elderly woman passes Matt on the street and gives him a suspicious look. He lowers his voice to a whisper. "Never fear, fearless leader. I'm on the scent."

"Matt, you're starting to sound like an international spy."

"Bond's the name. Today I take my first ride on a surfboard. Wish me luck."

Matt hangs up. Thousands of miles away his mentor scratches a pen across the page. The light outside the window is fading but a course of action is becoming clear: *Somebody needs to forge a successful marriage between Single Payer and Free Market.*

CHAPTER THREE

FREE MONEY?

In the center of Washington D.C., just beyond the shadow of the National Gallery of Art, in a park that hosts a looming sculpture of Supreme Court Justice Marshall, there is a life-size replica of two men playing chess on a bench. Just beyond this, on a similar bench, two real-life players concentrate over a chessboard. They enjoy an Indian Summer, but winter is beginning to make itself known. Asleep on a farther bench, a homeless man snores inside his cocoon of filthy coats, newspapers and blankets.

The younger of the chess players, Kristina, moves her knight, blows warm air on her cold fingers and tugs on a pair of gloves. "Cold day."

"Bad play," responds her partner, Carl. "I'll have checkmate in fourteen moves."

"Uncle Carl! How do you do that!" Kristina slaps a gloved hand on the cement bench, knowing full well how her uncle does it. Gifted with a mind like a friendly computer, he is a chief analyst at the Treasury Department and looks the part, with his high forehead and wire-rimmed glasses, his translucent skin and tailored, vested suit.

Carl smiles as he clears the chessboard and leans back to clean his lenses. "I just like to think ahead to see what's going to happen."

Though a less magnificent chess player, Kristina is no slouch in the intellectual arena. On a fast track to becoming a high-powered attorney, she switched gears suddenly to pursue the path of public service, then switched back again, drawn by the money. She happens to have a close friend—a very close friend—named Matt.

Kristina watches Carl clear the chess pieces, unzips her Gucci briefcase, pulls out a heavy document and drops it onto the bench. *Thunk!*

Carl looks down. "And what have we here?"

Kristina smiles mysteriously. "I wouldn't be bringing this up except that our mutual friend who is also my significant other is slumming around on the west coast, engaged in highly confidential research—last night on the telephone he called me 'dude.'"

Carl chuckles. "How is Matt?"

"Honestly? Obsessed with nominating a certain someone for President."

"And I am in full accord. Most likely, the next president of our nation will be one who can deliver a solution to the healthcare crisis. I want it to be the HSA. But, if I'm not mistaken, you could care less who gets into office; you just want your money stream to keep flowing uninterrupted."

"Cruel yet correct. But I promised I'd help, and he sent me this fat, unattractive barge of data. Don't make such a face, Uncle Carl. Far too much paper has been wasted on healthcare. What we really need is *one* piece of paper, some genius to untangle the mass of arguments and opinions—or so says Matt."

"Can't argue that."

"Well, then. You people up at Treasury wrote the guidelines for this thing called the HSA, now John Q. Public needs a translation."

Carl is enigmatic, as always. Silent for a moment, as if considering his next chess move, he finally says, "It'll cost you dinner—at a very expensive restaurant."

Kristina hoists the five-pound document and lets it drop with its tell-tale thunk. "I'll pay anything to keep from having to chew through all this on my own."

They stand to go. Yards away, the homeless man stirs from sleep with a groan and shuffles his gray mass into a seated position. He calls out to Carl and Kristina in a poverty-roughened voice, "Spare some change?"

Carl immediately digs in his pocket, but Kristina holds back.

"Hey, Nasfiq," says Carl, stepping forward, "good to see you back on your feet. Take this and get something warm to eat—my niece will do the honors next time."

Kristina stiffens at the subtle jibe.

"Don't be late," mutters homeless Nasfiq, turning to Kristina with a wink. "That last move of yours? Moving your pawn instead of the knight could have saved you."

Later that night, at her brownstone in Georgetown, Kristina surfs the Web. Everyone seems to have an opinion on healthcare: Conservatives, Democrats, Republicans, Progressives, Libertarians, neo-Liberals, neo-Conservatives. All sides pose interesting arguments but basically there are two camps: those who want universal health coverage, a single-payer system with the government paying all the bills, and those who support consumer-directed healthcare, including the HSA.

But Kristina sees the tides changing as a growing number of Democrats take a second look at the HSA and find much to admire. *Hmm,* she thinks, *the two great political forces in America agreeing on something? Dinner with Uncle Carl will be worth the price of admission.*

Foosh-wup! A single page of paper drops down onto her dinner plate. Kristina takes her seat and looks at her uncle. "And what is this?"

"Exactly what you requested, my demanding niece: the Treasury Department's guidelines for the Health Savings Accounts. One piece of paper, delivered by a genius."

Kristina laughs and admires her surroundings, the gracious, inviting restaurant. "You got us my favorite table, Uncle Carl."

"Only the best will do."

"Right. Especially since I'm paying."

An attractive young Russian woman asks, "You will have drinks?"

Kristina looks at Uncle Carl. "Yes, in fact, we will," he responds. "Because it is my niece's money, I am tempted to order the Chateau Margaux '61, or another favorite, an early California vintage—organic, no sulfites—*but* we have a lot of work to do tonight, so I'm suggesting a couple of Arnold Palmers."

The server frowns, uncomprehending.

"Lovely," says Kristina, "just what I'm in the mood for, golfer's iced tea and lemonade." She turns to the young woman. "Bring the man his beverage. I'll stick to my Bombay Sapphire—up, please, with an olive." She turns back to Carl. "Enlighten me, now, dear Uncle. What is the meaning of this single-page, secret document?" Elegantly, she folds and unfolds the simple brochure resting on her plate.

Carl takes a long sip of his Arnold Palmer. "You want the executive summary—from the Treasury's perspective—regarding healthcare? A mess, a tangle. In the last ten years, a confusing bundle of coverage for catastrophic care, office visits, prescription drugs, labs and X-rays. The Treasury's solution? Strip it all down and define a bare bones approach. Voila. The HSA-qualified, high-deductible health plan."

"No bells and whistles, huh?"

"Precisely. Simple, catastrophic coverage. In our jargon, the HDHP."

"Exciting name."

"I'll ignore that. The Treasury expects consumers to save 20 to 60 percent over traditional HMO and PPO premiums, differences varying from company to company, state to state. Sort of like buying a car stripped of extras. Take away the leather seats, the fancy interior, the stereo system—and save a bundle."

"But everyone in this town wants fanny warmers, black-out windows and a global positioning system."

"And they pay for it, dear niece. Congress, the Treasury and the IRS would prefer you save your money, and in a specific way."

"Which money are we talking about now?"

"The premium savings. We're talking catastrophic insurance coverage. Did I lose you completely?"

"I'm just playing with you, Uncle Carl."

"It will come back to haunt you next Wednesday over the chess board—may we resume our discussion of the HSA?"

"You have my full attention." Kristina withdraws her olive from its bath of gin, enjoys a quiet nibble and reads where Carl is pointing.

Health Savings Accounts

A Health Savings Account (HSA) is an account that you can put money into to save for future medical expenses. There are certain advantages to putting money into these accounts, including favorable tax treatment. HSAs were signed into law by President Bush on December 8, 2003.

Who Can Have an HSA

Any adult can contribute to an HSA if they:

- Have coverage under an HSA-qualified "high-deductible health plan" (HDHP)
- Have no other first-dollar medical coverage (other types of insurance like specific injury insurance or accident, disability, dental care, vision care, or long term care insurance are permitted).
- Are not enrolled in Medicare.
- Cannot be claimed as a dependent on someone else's tax return.

"As you well know," says Carl, "when Uncle Sam wants the American people to behave in a certain way, he tempts them with tax benefits. For example, Uncle Sam wants you to save for retirement; therefore, contributions to your 401k or IRA are tax deductible and grow tax-free until retirement, at which time you must pay the taxes. But the HSA goes a step further. You don't pay taxes when you withdraw the money."

"Wait. What?"

The lovely Russian returns. "You will want food?"

"Ah, yes," says Carl, eyes lighting. "I'm nixing the Chilean sea bass—endangered species. And no veal—cruelty to young animals. The Kobe beef is too expensive—shipped halfway around the world and again, ignoble treatment of a noble beast. I recommend my niece have the cod—accessible and affordable and fished from local waters. For myself, I'll have portabella mushrooms in savory rosemary and garlic, a plate of heirloom tomatoes with asparagus—lightly grilled, if you will—and a salad of endive, radicchio and romaine hearts with a dusting of thyme and fresh chives."

"And I'll have filet mignon—rare." Kristina leans forward as she positions her napkin on her lap. "Now, back to the money. Did I hear you say *tax-free*?"

"You did. A triple tax benefit." Carl refers to a section of the brochure.

Tax Savings—An HSA provides you with triple tax savings:

1) Tax deduction when you contribute to your account,
2) tax-free earnings through investment, and
3) tax-free withdrawals for qualified medical expenses.

"When you or your employer opens an HSA at a local bank or financial institution, Uncle Sam cannot touch it; this is *tax deductible*. As the money grows and earns interest, Uncle Sam cannot touch it; this is your *tax-free growth*. And when you spend the money on healthcare, again, Uncle Sam can't touch it; these are your *tax-free withdrawals*.

"Typically, before you receive your paycheck, your employer deducts taxes. If you are an average American, this is about 25%. For every thousand dollars of your paycheck, your employer deducts at least one-fourth, or $250, in taxes, and you receive the balance. If you have a $1,000 medical bill, you have to earn $1,333, give $333 to Uncle Sam, and then pay the doctor. The real cost, then, is not the amount of the bill but the cost of what you have to earn. However, if you have an HSA, you avoid paying $333 to Uncle Sam. For every thousand dollars of medical expenses you incur over a lifetime, you'll save $333 each time.

"Most Americans believe that tax breaks are only for the wealthy, but the HSA is here to change that, to give tax incentives to all the workforce of America. In other words, money untouched by Uncle Sam."

"And why isn't everyone jumping for joy?"

"They are. It is the fastest growing trend in the history of health insurance—but the Treasury has put strict limits on how much you can deposit into these accounts."

"How high can I go? Does your little brochure tell me?" Kristina lifts the tri-fold Treasury brochure and squints at the information.

"What do you know. Here it is."

HSA Contributions.

You can make a contribution to your HSA each year that you are eligible. You can contribute up to the amount of your HDHP deductible but no more than:

$2,850* – Self-only coverage

$5,650* – Family coverage

*2007 amounts; adjusted annually for inflation.

Individuals age 55 and older can also make additional "catch-up" contributions. The maximum annual catch-up contribution is as follows:

2006	$700
2007	$800
2008	$900
2009 and after	$1,000

Contributions to your HSA can be made by you, your employer or both. However, the total contributions are limited annually. If you make a contribution, you can deduct the contributions (even if you do not itemize deductions) when completing your federal income tax return.

Contributions to the account must stop once you are enrolled in Medicare. However, you can keep the money in your account and use it to pay for medical expenses tax-free.

"From the looks of this, I am rewarded for good health with money?"

Carl nods. "Read the next paragraph."

Using Your HSA

You can use the money in the account to pay for any "qualified medical expense" permitted under federal tax law. This includes most medical care and services, and dental and vision care, and also includes over-the-counter drugs such as aspirin.

You can generally not use the money to pay for medical insurance premiums, except under specific circumstances, including:

- Any health plan coverage while receiving federal or state unemployment benefits.

- COBRA continuation coverage after leaving employment with a company that offers health insurance coverage.
- Qualified long-term care insurance.
- Medicare premiums and out-of-pocket expenses, including deductibles, co-pays, and coinsurance for:
    * Part A (hospital and inpatient services)
    * Part B (physician and outpatient services)
    * Part C (Medicare HMO and PPO plans)
    * Part D (Prescription drugs)

"Is this telling me what I think it is? This HSA is like a big benevolent octopus with financial arms everywhere. I can use HSA dollars to pay for health expenses in retirement not covered by Medicare? Brilliant," she says, sitting back in her chair and looking directly into Carl's eyes. "Everyone in my age group should demand this plan from their employers. Plan and save for the future while our health is good and expenses are low. You know, Uncle Carl, we don't trust Medicare to be there when we need it. Not to be cynical, but your generation has thoroughly complicated social services."

Carl's eyes twinkle. "And we're trying to redeem ourselves. We're very proud of our work over at the Department. But take a look at this…we're especially proud of this." Carl taps his finger and Kristina reads:

> You can use your money in the account to pay for medical expenses for yourself, your spouse, or your dependent children. You can pay for expenses of your spouse or dependent children even if they are not covered by your HDHP.

Kristina looks up. "This HSA is very user-friendly. If you had uninsurable family members, you could use the HSA to pay their medical bills."

Carl beams. "Read on."

> Any amounts used for purposes other than to pay for "qualified medical expenses" are taxable as income and subject to an additional 10% tax penalty. Examples include:
>
> - Medical expenses that are not considered "qualified medical expenses" under federal tax law (e.g., cosmetic surgery).
> - Other types of health insurance unless specifically described above.

- Medicare supplement insurance premiums
- Expenses that are not medical or health related.
- After you turn age 65, or if you become disabled, the 10% additional tax penalty no longer applies.

"No wonder Matt is extolling this as a possible healthcare solution for America."

"Here's the coup de gráce," Carl adds. "At age 65 your unused dollars can be used for non-medical expenses during retirement, taxed like an IRA. Congress hopes when consumers spend their own dollars, they will shop for the best values and save money instead of over-utilizing the healthcare system."

"HSA dollars for doctor visits, prescriptions drugs, annual exams, labs and X-rays? But how do I use this thing? Let's say I go to the doctor and need a prescription?"

"Pull out your HSA debit card and pay right on the spot. The money is automatically deducted from your account."

"Or I need an MRI?"

"Go for it—use your HSA checkbook."

"Or, let's say I hate doctors. Let's say I only believe in acupuncture?"

"HSA, all the way."

"What if I need eyeglasses?—contacts?—LASIK surgery?"

"HSA dollars, all of them."

"Date with a dental hygienist for a simple cleaning?"

"Yes."

"Braces for my kids?"

Carl raises an eyebrow. "*Kids*?"

"How about toothache? Root canal?"

"Yes, but may we move away from the mouth? I'm rather enjoying my dinner."

"What if I want to lose weight, learn better nutrition, get buffed out?"

"All but the last. You can use HSA dollars to pay for visits to a dietician or nutritionist and for all prescribed vitamins and supplements but not for the actual groceries. Likewise, use your HSA for an exercise physiologist to write out an optimum exercise program, but not—"

"—to pay for a membership to the gym."

"Hear, hear. Here's the general formula: tax-free HSA dollars may legally be used to pay for prevention, diagnosis and treatment by a healthcare professional."

"Can I pay my health insurance premiums with it?"

"Did you not read the fine print? Health insurance premiums are specifically excluded except in the case of long-term care insurance premiums."

"Why?"

"When the government wants to encourage the citizens—"

Kristina grins. "They give a tax incentive."

"Brilliant. Long-term care for we baby boomers has the potential to bankrupt the government, so we get a tax break here."

"How about plastic surgery?"

"Reconstructive, yes. Cosmetic, no."

"What if I have a common cold? Do over-the-counter medications count?"

"Absolutely."

"What if Washington is stressing me, and I need a therapist?"

"That's treatment, isn't it? By all means, pay her with your HSA dollars."

Kristina takes the time to thoroughly study the Treasury brochure, this time with the aid of her reading glasses.

> **Advantages of HSAs**
>
> **Security**—Your high deductible insurance and HSA protect you against high or unexpected medical bills.

Affordability—You should be able to lower your health insurance premiums by switching to health insurance coverage with a higher deductible.

Flexibility—You can use the funds in your account to pay for current medical expenses including expenses that your insurance may not cover, or save the money in your account for future needs, such as:

- Health insurance or medical expenses if unemployed
- Medical expenses after retirement (before Medicare)
- Out-of-pocket expenses when covered by Medicare
- Long-term care expenses and insurance

Savings—You can save the money in your account for future medical expenses and grow your account through investment earnings.

Control—You make all the decisions about:

- How much money to put into the account
- Whether to save the account for future expenses or pay current medical expenses
- Which medical expenses to pay from the account
- Which company will hold the account
- Whether to invest any of the money in the account
- Which investments to make

Portability—Accounts are completely portable, meaning you can keep your HSA even if you:

- Change jobs
- Change your medical coverage
- Become unemployed
- Move to another state
- Change your marital status

Ownership—Funds remain in the account from year to year, just like an IRA. There are no "use it or lose it" rules for HSAs.

"Uncle Carl, this is a watershed idea. Even if I change jobs, I retain my full Health Savings Account." Kristina refolds the brochure and slips it into her handbag with a smile. "One page delivered by a genius."

Carl grins, and the young Russian returns to ask, "You will take dessert?"

"Yes," laughs Kristina. "Something succulent, decadent and expensive—and a pot of very hot coffee."

"Herbal tea for me," adds Carl, and Kristina launches in with, "Well, my good uncle, if I understand, HSAs will cover acupuncture, alcoholism, arch supports, Braille books, chiropractors, Christian Science practitioners, crutches, dentures, drug addiction, eyeglasses, guide dogs, MRIs, legal fees, organ transplants, osteopaths, pediatricians, post-nasal treatments, psychiatrists, transplants, vitamins, wheelchairs, wigs—"

Carl grins. "That's about half of it—what? What's wrong? Your lovely face has fallen."

"I'm not a bad person, Uncle Carl," says Kristina behind tears, "I just love what money can do."

"I never said you were, my dear."

"I do have a heart, it's just buried." She dips into her Prada for a Kleenex.

"Of course you do. I never doubted it. Precisely why Matt adores you."

Kristina heaves a sigh and looks intently at her uncle. "I can't help wondering. What about Nasfiq? What's this system going to do for him?"

"Why do you think Matt is flying around the country on behalf of our presidential hopeful? If our politicians—if we ourselves—are not leaders with brave hearts, we are doomed. The working poor must be drawn into the circle—and the needy."

Kristina wipes her eyes delicately with the tissue. "Absolutely… and the truly needy."

* * * * * * *

Matt is on his cell phone to D.C. "I've got a question, boss. We do all of our business in Washington, D.C., and I'm out here doing all of my research on the Left Coast?"

"That's easy. California is always at the forefront of change in health insurance."

"So...the person I really need to talk to is...a California insurance agent?"

"Or send in a good investigative reporter."

"I know someone. She's sharp. She's also in a wheelchair with health complications."

"I'm so sorry. I always hate to hear that."

"Yeah. Shouldn't happen to anyone, not at her age. I'll see if she wants the assignment."

"How are we doing otherwise?"

"Honestly?" responds Matt. He drops his sunglasses on the warm sand and bends to retrieve them. Thirty feet away a dozen women compete in an impromptu game of beach volleyball. "Honestly? This HSA seems to be popping up everywhere."

"That's a good thing."

"Yep," chirps Matt. "Have you read about Wal-Mart? Course you have. They're stepping in to follow the money."

"Establishing their own banks and health savings accounts, offering HDHPs and HSAs to new employees—is that what you mean?—Matt, you seem a little distracted—anything wrong on your end?"

"Huh? No." Matt rushes over to retrieve an out-of-bounds volleyball, handing it with a grin to a grateful volleyball player. "Huh? No, no, I'm right here. Wal-Mart. They're setting up mini-clinic pilot programs. You'll be able to go to Wal-Mart, eat your hot dog, stop by the mini-clinic to see why your tummy is rumbling, go to the pharmacist for your acid reflux prescription, and pay for it with your Wal-Mart HSA—without leaving the parking lot."

"And," adds Matt's mentor, "these low-cost clinics are open at hours when moms can bring in their sick children before school or talk in person to a healthcare provider after the late shift. A no-appointment visit for only $25."

"How about Dial-a-Doc? Heard of them? Another entrepreneurial whiz. You call a doctor. She listens to your symptoms, asks questions and guides you to appropriate action. She'll have electronic records and a history of all of your medical problems, treatments and prescriptions."

"Hm. What's the cost on that?"

"Thirty-five bucks and up."

"And Aetna Insurance pioneered that price transparency program, and all the companies are following suit. The average citizen wasn't getting simple answers when they asked clinics or doctors or hospitals, 'How much does this really cost?'"

"Oh, yeah, I read about that," says Matt, watching with regret as the volleyball game breaks up. "Consumers log onto the computer and compare physicians by quality, service and price. Which is good because, in the past, insurance companies held the money and made the decisions. With HSAs in the hands of the consumers, entrepreneurial innovation will inspire new products and services…except, no one's mentioning the big fat pink elephant in the living room."

The legislator is thoughtful. "No one wants to think about the desperately poor, the needy and the uninsurable. It makes their pretty formulas go haywire."

"How'd you know?"

He can hear the smile at the other end. "Matt…I'm in this business for a reason."

"I'll say: the far-seeing gaze of the great politician."

"I prefer to think of myself as an enlightened governor of the people's wishes."

"On you, it works. Hey—ever try surfing? You should…you really should."

"*The eternity of the ocean? The infinity of the wave?*"

"Wow, how'd you know?"

"Gotta go now, Matt. Get in touch with your investigative reporter. Our time is crunching to a close."

Matt salutes involuntarily, “At your service, oh great, wise one.”

He hears a sigh imbedded in the laughter from the other end. “Matt—you really do belong out there. You’re about as Left Coast as a Washingtonian can be.”

“You got that right dude.”

“Your royal highness dude, to you,” the candidate says, with a grin.

Matt hangs up, laughing.

CHAPTER FOUR

Searching for the Silver Bullet

Monday morning, dark-haired Lorellei sits in her personal cubicle in the noisy newsroom of the small local newspaper. The UPS carrier drops a heavy cardboard mailer on her desk with a thunk. Struggling to reach for it, Lorellei shifts her weight, and pain shoots up her legs like needles. She grimaces, as much in frustration as in pain, and sits back gingerly.

Last night on the phone with Matt she accepted his assignment, planning to moonlight during one of her lunch hours and interview the owner of some local insurance agency. Maybe she'll turn around and sell the idea to her own editor, a nice glossy supplement to the Sunday edition of the paper, something along the lines of *Healthcare Solutions: From the Horse's Mouth*. Late in the day, the office gofer slides a memo across her desk. She welcomes the interruption. "Afternoon, Derek, what's up?"

"Oh, man, yer not gonna like this one. Everybody's mad at me. I'm the Santa Claus of Doom—see ya."

Lorellei watches him pad lightly away and hears the slap as the memo hits each desk, followed by audible groaning. Her dark eyes settle on the heading at the top of the memo, Changes in Employee Contributions to Health Insurance, and she reads on.

> Due to increases in costs, at open enrollment we will be adjusting the current benefits plan and inviting you to participate freely in this challenging combination of copays and coinsurance. Please attend this Friday's informational meeting!
>
> All employees may keep their current benefit structure, with an additional 25% employee contribution.

Lorellei rocks back in her seat. *A twenty-five percent increase? If I choose to keep my current benefits?* Her spine cramps in response, and she reminds herself to keep calm. The binder from Matt seems to be staring at her. When the suppleness returns to her hands she rummages in her bottom drawer and turns the yellow pages to a bold ad for Health Savings Accounts and a friendly photograph of "The HSA Crusader."

Corny, thinks Lorellei—*corny but perfect.* Matt needs an expert in the field of insurance, with a focus on Health Savings Accounts—whatever they might be—and she now has a personal incentive. The newspaper has always provided full health coverage for its employees—benefits she makes good use of. But now her "free" insurance is suddenly slipping away. Why? Maybe the HSA Crusader can shed some light.

The clock eventually ticks to quitting time. She slips into a sweater and, releasing the brakes on her wheelchair, slides down the handicap ramp to the parking lot outside.

That night, while Lorellei scans Matt's document, her husband Sydney browses Health Savings Accounts on the Web and is bombarded with 8,990,000 citations. He spools through hundreds of newspaper and magazine articles. "...This is happening in companies all across America...banks are getting on board...physicians are supporting this system...and to think I never heard of the things before tonight."

"I haven't been paying attention," admits Lorellei sheepishly, "but it looks like an underground issue getting ready to explode."

"Looks like it's already exploded," muses Sydney, rubbing his hands together. "Maybe we should get on board."

"It can't help me, locked into my employer—literally—for the benefits I receive."

Sydney smoothly lifts Lori from the wheelchair. "It's late. Time to rest. We'll work something out." He heads down the hall, hiding his expression of concern.

The next day, before Lorellei has a chance to call the Crusader, the Human Resources director of the newspaper is working on her own insurance agenda. Inga Entemann has been in charge of HR for five years and dreads the upcoming enrollment period for their health plan. Each year as premiums increase the newspaper absorbs the mounting costs. But last year the CFO banged his fist on the desk and yelled, "I need a silver bullet to shoot down these premiums!" What will he do this year with a proposed 25% increase?

Inga rolls her eyes and squeezes into the narrow kitchen shared by all employees. Pouring herself a fresh cup of coffee, she reflects.

She certainly has not found her boss's silver bullet, and already the hallways are filled with grumbling in foreboding of this Friday's informational meeting. How can she face a room full of employees for the sixth year in a row, smiling and painting a rosy picture? They won't want to hear about healthcare inflation rocketing at two to three times the normal inflation rate. Nor will they turn a happy ear when she explains that everyone needs to share the rising costs, with all of them paying more and getting less.

An employee herself, she feels the pinch, but she also sees the huge check her employer sends monthly to the insurance company to pay the group premium. And the worst irony, she thinks, cringing as she burns her tongue on the hot coffee, is that, other than Lorellei, most employees rarely use their full benefits.

The intercom calls her to the phone, and she answers to a vaguely familiar voice. Every year she entertains the quotes of various brokers to make sure her company is receiving the best value for its premium dollars. Dave, the man on the line, is one of these. He calls himself the HSA Crusader. Half-teasing, half-taunting, she asks, "Still on your crusade? You insurance people will do anything to squeeze more money from the unsuspecting consumer, won't you?"

She is surprised when Dave laughs heartily. "Just between you and me, Inga, I'm not the squeezer. HSA-Qualified HDHP premiums are 20 to 60% less than traditional PPOs and HMOs, and so are the commissions. With the HDHP, I make less money, you save more."

"You have nuts in your noggin. Why are you so enthusiastic?"

"Why wouldn't I be? With an HDHP to protect you from large and unexpected medical bills, and an HSA to pay routine expected expenses, you get to determine the future of your own healthcare. With good health you accrue savings you can use for the rest of your life, but after twenty years with a PPO you have nothing to show for it."

Remaining polite, Inga evades him, but his logic is still ringing in her ear the next day when her company's longtime insurance broker meets with her to deliver the final paperwork for their enrollment, confirming the 25% increase with a blank face.

But Inga is not so neutral. "Do you want to know what I think? I think it is highway robbery!" A flame rises in her cheeks. The broker hands her the renewal contract to sign, but she demurs. "Let me run this past Mr. Bradley one more time. I'll get back to you," she says with authority. She watches the smug broker retreat down the hall, knowing he doesn't mind the rising costs—his commission is fatter for it. Something in his manner convinces her to pick up her telephone and dial Dave. "E-mail everything you have," she tells him. "All the numbers...everything."

Forty-five minutes later, Inga quietly closes her door to read the e-mail.

> Thanks for the opportunity to present material for your eighteen employees. You will reap substantial savings by switching from your PPO and HMO plans to a high-deductible health plan for all your employees. Those savings in premiums transfer directly into a health savings account for each employee, empowering them to care for their own routine expected healthcare while saving for future expenses. I call this the HSA Strategy. You will find (with pleasure, I'm guessing) that the large majority of your employees are able to save a nice chunk of money each year in their HSA—money they get to keep! Please call with any questions.

Glancing at the chart on the second page, Inga's glance moves immediately to the bottom line. *High-deductible health plans for about half the cost of the other two plans?* Compared to the PPO plan, which is most popular among the newspaper's employees, the savings is $9,795, almost $10,000 per month!

PPO	HMO	**HDHP**
$17,025	$16,290	**$7,230**

	Traditional PPO	Traditional HMO	HDHP
Benefits			
Type of plan	PPO	HMO	PPO
Deductible	$250	$0	$3,000/$6,000
Office visit	$20	$10	0% after deductible
Outpatient services	20%	No charge	0% after deductible
Hospital	20%	No charge	0% after deductible
Out-of-network	40%	Emergency only	50% after deductible

	Traditional PPO	Traditional HMO	HDHP
Rx-generic	$15	$10	$0 after deductible
Rx-brand name	$25	$20	$0 after deductible
Individual Max OOP	$3,000	$1,750	$3,000
Family max OOP	$6,000	$3,500	$6,000
Employee only	PPO $20 ($)	HMO $100 ($)	HDHP ($)
#1 20-29	240	265	100
#2 30-39	310	340	135
#3 40-49	410	370	200
#4 50-54	545	470	235
#5 55-59	670	590	305
#6 60-64	865	785	380
Employee + spouse			
#7 20-29	715	690	210
#8 30-39	845	825	280
#9 40-49	840	905	405
#10 50-54	1,140	935	495
#11 55-59	1,410	1,315	625
#12 60-64	1,725	1,445	765
Employee + family			
#13 20-29	805	885	290
#14 30-39	930	1,040	380
#15 40-49	1,025	1,115	490
#16 50-54	1,215	1,250	515
#17 55-59	1,475	1,385	650
#18 60-64	1,860	1,680	770
Monthly totals	**$17,025**	**$16,290**	**$7,230**

Inga taps her calculator, subtracting $7,230 from $17,025.

Dave's HSA Strategy proposes her company contribute this $9,795 to HSAs rather than pay premiums for office visits and prescription drug copays. This amounts to $544 per month saved for each employee.

Hm, this could purchase a lot of healthcare. And each employee is empowered to use that money to shop for their own healthcare values. She stares at the ceiling. That's $544 per employee. Is this accurate?

She reads more of Dave's Treasury material and learns there are limits to monthly contributions.

> HSA legislation says that you can put 100% of your deductible into an HSA, not to exceed a certain maximum.*

Inga scans down to the fine print.

> *$2,850 for individuals and $5,650 for families in 2007.

Not bad, she thinks. *That ought to cover everything that isn't a full-blown disaster.* She continues to read, thinking, *Since the deductible for the company's six single employees would be $3,000 each, this allows $2,850 per year into each single employee's HSA. The twelve employees with spouses can deposit $5,650 of their $6,000 family aggregate deductible into their HSA—money in the bank.*

Money Going into Employee HSAs		
# of employees	**Monthly contribution per employee ($)**	**Total monthly contribution ($)**
6 single	237	1,422
6 w/ spouse	470	2,820
6 w/ family	470	2,820
Total of 18 employees		**$7,062/month**

Inga reviews. *The allowable contribution is $7,062 for all the employees, and we have already saved $9,795, which, minus $7,062 is...* Her lips form a silent *wow*. After funding all employee health savings accounts, and after paying all of their high deductible insurance, the company experiences a net savings of $2,733 per month! She sits up in her chair. *Over thirty-two thousand per year! The CFO is going to love this. His silver bullet! And administration of the HSA Strategy will be much easier than traditional health plans.*

- The broker will conduct educational classes to explain how the plan works and how all employees will benefit, and will then enroll all employees.
- Every month, accounting sends a check to the insurance company to pay the HDHP premiums and another check to a financial institution where the money is distributed into each employee's HSA.

- The employees will each have an HSA debit card and/or a checkbook to pay routine expected medical bills. Employees will be able to access their HSA account online and manage how HSA dollars are invested, just like they do with a 401(k) plan.

Excited, daring to hope, Inga hurries to the final chart.

The HSA Strategy—A Lifetime of Better Health		
Steps		
	BEFORE RETIREMENT	
1	**Enroll** in an affordable HDHP to protect against large unexpected medical bills.	When you switch from a traditional HMO or low deductible PPO to the HDHP, you will save 20-60% on premiums.
2	**Open** an HSA to pay routine expected medical expenses and save for future deductibles.	Use premium savings to fund HSA; contribute additional money to maximize annual HSA contribution. Most people will have unused dollars to roll into next year.
3a	**Use** tax-free HSA dollars to maximize health.	HSA dollars pay for current medical, dental, vision, alternative care, prescriptions, as well as health education to improve wellness.
3b	**Set a goal** to save and invest unused HSA dollars to provide a lifetime of benefits.	HSA dollars can fund future expenses that occur before retirement, retirement healthcare expenses not covered by Medicare, long term care premiums and any final expenses.
	AT RETIREMENT	Have two separate sources of money for retirement expenses: Tax-free HSA dollars for healthcare and IRA, 401(k), pension & social security for daily living.
4	**Create** a stream of income for retirement healthcare expenses.	Instead of reinvesting HSA returns, create a monthly stream of tax-free income to pay routine expected expenses not paid by Medicare.

The HSA Strategy—A Lifetime of Better Health		
5	**Buy** a low-cost, high-deductible Medicare supplement, if available in your state, and save on monthly premiums.	With your pool of HSA dollars, feel comfortable buying a high-deductible Medicare supplement. Use your HSA dollars to pay the deductibles.
6	**Pay** LTC insurance premiums.	Use the interest from your HSA investments to pay LTC premiums.
7	**Pay** un-reimbursed LTC expenses.	Use your HSA to supplement what is not covered or, if you don't have an LTC policy, to pay the cost of long-term care.
8	**Have a reserve** if Medicare is reduced or restricted.	If Medicare substantially increases Part A and B deductibles or restricts eligibility, an HSA can be a reserve of money to pay costs that would have been covered by Medicare.
9	If necessary, **supplement your retirement income** (with the withdrawals taxed like IRA funds).	It is best to use your HSA primarily for healthcare expenses and, if necessary, as a source for monthly living expenses.
	AFTER PASSING ON	
10	**Give funds** to your spouse.	At your death, if your spouse is your HSA beneficiary, HSA dollars roll over tax-free into your spouse's HSA.
11	**Bequeath** it to your heirs (with funds taxed like IRA funds).	Include instructions for heirs to use the money for their HSA.
12	**Pay** final expenses (with funds taxed like IRA funds).	After-tax expenses such as burial, cremation and debts can be paid instead of burdening family.

Armed with Dave's ammunition, Inga is ready to meet with CFO Bradley and is freshening her lipstick when seized with a wave of doubt. *What about Lorellei's ongoing problems? Mr. Bradley is going to ask some pretty sharp questions, the first of which will be, 'Will the HSA plan work for Lorellei?'*

* * * * * * *

A bright window reveals fragrant cherry blossoms that will soon explode with perfume. Matt eagerly takes the wingchair across the desk from his mentor and flashes a surfer's smile. "Reporting for duty, dude. Are you ready to announce your candidacy? Ready to sail the great ship of state—the USS Healthcare?"

The legislator, whose winter has been the long scrabbling give-and-take of Washington, defers with an appreciative chuckle. "We have not yet found the miracle to unite the nation. Our wide array of political factions seem at war. There are those who want things just as they are..."

Matt rolls his eyes.

"...and single-payer advocates want Uncle Sam to take care of everything, which will cause tax brackets to rise an additional 10% to 20%—whether you need medical care or not. At the other extreme, some advocate keeping the government entirely out of healthcare—get rid of all social services and taxes. Then you have the HDHP-HSA model, where healthy people enjoy the financial advantage of good health and unhealthy people have the benefit of affording medical bills, but there are some gaping holes."

Matt shapes his hands into a megaphone, mocking a Hollywood producer. "Ah, yes, the great ship of state remains afloat but she's taken some hits...the USS Healthcare headed into monstrous seas. Will she capsize? Will those on board survive?"

Across the desk, Matt's mentor chuckles. "You know, I think California has its hooks in you. You might want to consider a career in the movie industry."

"Thanks but I'll stick to politics—much more intrigue."

They sit quietly for a moment, the legislator making notes. Matt loses himself in dreamland for a moment, then blurts, "You know Australia and New Zealand? They've always had national healthcare funded by government, but people want private health plans. Which means, if you figure it out for good old Uncle Sam, we might be onto a global solution."

CHAPTER FIVE

WILL IT WORK FOR ME?

Sydney wheels Lorellei through a beautiful courtyard with picturesque Italian fountains and swaying palm trees. It is California at its best but just as easily might be a lively town on the Mediterranean coast. Lorellei presses her husband's hand. "Nice setting."

They enter a courtyard office and approach David, the HSA Crusader, whose hand is extended in friendship. Six-and-a-half feet tall, he outstrips Sydney by about three inches, but there is nothing aggressive in his demeanor. He looks like the amiable chemistry professor at a Midwestern college. He greets them with an easy smile. "I'm David—call me Dave—and you must be Sydney and *Lora... Loral... Lorally*?

Lorellei laughs. "Close. No one gets it right the first time. The pronunciation is Spanish. You need to roll the R and pronounce the two Ls as a Y."

The HSA Crusader tries again—"LorrrrrreY-aye—?" and they laugh.

"Why don't you just call me Lori."

"Let's do that. I have a truck driver's finesse with foreign languages—so, what brings the two of you here today?" Dave glances at the wheelchair. His unavoidable, unvoiced thought? *This woman is uninsurable. I hope she's covered at her job.*

"Actually," says Lorellei, "I'm an investigative reporter."

"Oh, good," voices the HSA Crusader with some relief. "Why not take a seat here, Sydney, and you, Lori, snuggle that wheelchair in close so you can both see the computer monitor. Just what is it you're investigating?"

"Without wasting any breath? I want you to prove that health savings accounts are truly the solution for the health insurance crisis in America."

"Whoa! You *don't* waste any breath—and you've come to the right place. The HSA is my *raison d'être*, my passion, my star, my guiding light."

Whatever floats your boat, thinks Sydney.

As if the Crusader can read his mind, he turns to Sydney. "Honestly, I can talk all day, explaining Health Savings Accounts in great detail, but ultimately there is only one important question: will it work for you?"

"Well, it's clearly not going to work for me," says Lorellei abruptly, "not with my medical conditions. I saw that look on your face when I wheeled in here."

Like any good salesman, Dave demurs. "If I convince you this plan works for you, will it be sufficient argument to convince you it works for the rest of America?"

"It…might."

"And you, Sydney?" he says, surprising Lorellei's husband out of his thoughts. "What's your insurance story? Whatever you're thinking now, I guarantee you are going to feel more relaxed at the end of this meeting."

"I'll take the bait. What do you want to know? I'm in good health, self-employed, and buy my own health insurance. One chronic condition—hypertension, the scourge of the African-American—for which I take one prescription."

"Placing you in the 24% of Americans who regularly spend approximately $1,000 per year on healthcare."

Sydney lifts an eyebrow. "You guys are that sure of your statistics?"

"What can I say? Insurance actuaries spend their lives honing it down to the fine point. You probably take a brand-name prescription which costs about $80 per month and that's $960 per year. These are the *real* costs—not what you experience with your copay, mind you. If you were completely healthy, falling into the 68% of Americans who spend less than $500 per year, it would be a no-brainer. The HSA is always the best plan for that particular group—but I'll also prove it is best for you."

Turning to Lorellei, Dave softens his voice. "Lori, am I safe in assuming you have an ongoing, chronic condition requiring frequent doctor visits and prescriptions?"

"Yes. It manifested the year we got married. Rheumatoid arthritis." Lorellei looks down at her hands. "My mother and my grandmother had it before me."

"I'm sorry. It's a tough one."

"Mostly a battle with myself. If I stay away from stress and am really careful about what I eat and how I exercise, I actually do okay. But the regimen is challenging."

The Crusader can see the struggle behind her eyes. "I'm not a physician," he says. "I cannot prescribe any form of treatment, but I have someone with an inspiring story I'd like you to meet when we finish. She will give a little local color for your research."

"Oh, right, sure. When we finish here."

"Let's see now, Lori...your particular health challenge places you in the 8% of Americans who cost the insurance companies an average of $12,000 per year in healthcare expenses."

Lorellei takes a few notes, heaving an unwonted sigh. "Oh? I cost them that much? And my employer just hiked my rates 25%—but this interview isn't about me."

"Of course not, and I apologize on behalf of my industry for the rising rates, but it's happening everywhere—one of the myriad reasons I continue to shout from the rooftops about the HSA."

Dave looks from Sydney to Lorellei. He's met with thousands of people across this same desk. He's guessing this couple has been married no more than three years. Lorellei is bright and capable and braving out a terrible health problem. Strong, handsome Sydney is as frightened as a puppy behind that peaceful facade. His heart goes out to them, but the Crusader takes seriously his job to guide them professionally through the miasma of health insurance and keeps his voice brisk.

"Lorellei—Wow! I pronounced it correctly! My wife says I'm trainable. Let's use you as the test case to convince us of the merits of the HSA. What kind of plan do you currently have?"

"I'm insured with my company, Channel Daily News, and we have, let's see...it's Blue Sky Insurance."

The HSA Crusader's eyes grow large. Inga Entemann has just asked him to quote insurance rates for Channel Daily News, but he's pledged to confidentiality. "Do you have any specific idea how much your company pays for you every month?"

"Hm. Well, no, actually. Until now, my employer paid everything."

"That's fair. What kind of copay do you have for doctor visits?"

"I pay $20 each time."

The Crusader flips through a stack of papers on his desk and pulls out a chart.

Blue Sky Insurance Company: Plan Options (2-50 employees)			
Plan Features	**HMO**	**PPO with low deductible**	**HDHP**
Deductible	0	$250	$3,000 individual $6,000 family
Coinsurance (Amount you pay after deductible)	0%	20%	0%
Out-of-pocket maximum (Total paid including deductible)	0	$3,000	$3,000 individual $6,000 family
Office visits (Copays not subject to deductible)	$10 copay	**$20 copay**	Pay full fee
Prescription brand-name drugs (Copays not subject to deductible)	$25 copay	$25 copay	Pay full fee
Annual exam (Office visit plus lab tests)	$100 copay	$100 copay	$100 copay

"Here's a spreadsheet with the most popular plans, including yours. Now, let's look at the rate book—and I'm just guessing, but I'll put you in the 30-39 year age range—and your husband is not insured with you?"

"Correct," says Lorellei.

"Okay. Let's look at this chart."

Blue Sky Insurance Premiums (Age-rated and in dollars)			
	PPO	**HMO**	**HDHP**
Single			
under 30	240	265	100
30-39	**310**	340	135
40-49	410	370	200
50-54	545	470	235
55-59	670	590	305
60-64	865	785	380

"To insure you, your employer spends $310 per month."

"I had no idea. Seems like a lot."

"Most employees have no idea what their employers pay for insurance. Let me guess…you probably see a doctor a dozen times—"

"—ten times a year, and I take five prescriptions. My rheumatologist told me if I paid full price they'd cost over five hundred per month. Lucky I have the $25 copay."

"*Lucky,* you say? What if we were to look at your *real* costs, here, and what if we were to find that your $25 copay is not what it seems?"

Lorellei and Sydney glance at each other and pay closer attention.

"Let's put the boxers in the ring, shall we? In one corner we place your current PPO and in the other corner the HDHP and HSA."

Dave scribbles intently, slanting the page for Lori and Sydney's eyes. "All right, let's look at the Blue Sky Insurance rate sheet—the one I *just* showed you. Boy, it's amazing how quickly things get lost on my desk."

Dave searches the top of his desk. "Okay, here we go. If you switch from the PPO costing $310 to the HDHP costing $135, you'll save $175 per month, which can be deposited into your HSA. After one year, your health savings account will accumulate $2,100, and this money can be used to pay any and all legitimate healthcare expenses.

"Currently, with your employer paying the full cost of your PPO, you don't feel any of this. It all goes on behind your back. With the

HSA, you would experience ownership of the $175 per month, but the actual HDHP insurance payments would still be made by your employer. Now let's isolate your *out-of-pocket costs*, which is insurance jargon for the 'ouch' of spending your own money. I'm guessing your specialist costs $120 per visit and you go ten times. Right now, with your $20 copay you only experience the 'ouch' of $200.

"Same thing with your prescriptions. Five prescriptions that each cost $100 per month total $500. Over twelve months that equals $6,000. Right now, with your copay, you only experience the 'ouch' of $1,500. So, adding your $200 in office visit copays with your $1,500 in brand-name prescription copays, the total annual 'ouch' for your current plan is $1,700."

"And," intrudes Lorellei, "if I were uninsured it would cost me $1,200 for office visits plus the $6,000 for prescriptions, or $7,200 per year."

Dave agrees. "True. If you didn't have insurance, you'd spend $7,200 per year. But with the HDHP, once you reach your $3,000 deductible, the insurance company pays the rest. At the most, all you would ever pay per year would be $3,000—not $7,200."

"So," announces Lorellei triumphantly, "the 'ouch' for my current copay plan is $1,700, and it would be $3,000 for your beloved HDHP? That's not a good deal."

Crusader Dave grins. "You're forgetting the sweet little HSA which now holds a reservoir of $2,100 deposited there by your employer. If we subtract that $2,100 from your $3,000 deductible, your 'ouch' factor with the HDHP-HSAs ends up being only $900 compared to how much for that 'wonderful' copay plan of yours?"

"Compared to $1,700." Lorellei sighs, sinking in her chair. "What can I say? Ouch. Even with my employer fully funding my current insurance, I am paying $800 more per year out of my own pocket than if I had the HDHP and an HSA. And I've been doing so for several years, always thinking I had the best possible deal."

"Amazing, isn't it? You only find the truth when you follow the money. And another comment here about 'free' insurance. This is from

Devon Herrick, health economist and senior fellow at the National Center of Policy Analysis:

> Employer-sponsored health coverage is popular because workers mistakenly assume their employers pay part of the premiums. Economists know otherwise. Workers bear the total cost of their health plans through direct contribution and indirect wage reductions.

Sydney sits forward. "Of course. If I were going to hire an employee for $20 per hour and he insisted on health insurance coverage, I'd take it out of his hourly pay. He would then effectively be getting, what?"

"About $18 per hour plus his coverage," finishes the Crusader. "What can I say? Nobody gets a free lunch. And since the funding for your premiums is ultimately your money, it is all the more important for you to have a say in which plan your employer chooses. Isn't it, Lorellei?"

"We've been thinking," says Sydney with a frown, "of trying those injections for arthritis? They're rumored to be very effective, but the cost is astronomical."

Dave nods. "It so happens I have a longtime client with arthritis. The series of injections costs around $30,000 per year. With Lorellei's current employer-funded prescription drug plan, she's required to pay 30% of the costs of any injections."

Sydney sits forward, incredulous. "That's nine thousand bucks she'd have to pay! Even with her employer's insurance!"

"Hold on—help is at hand. With the HDHP, once Lorellei meets the $3,000 deductible, insurance pays the rest. And once she subtracts that $2,100 out of her HSA, she ends up with an 'ouch' of $900."

"That's $900 versus $9,000?" Lorellei whispers, "for the entire yearly series of injections? Sign me up."

Dave smiles. "I thought this wasn't about you."

"Hey, I'm moonlighting as it is. Really, where's the dotted line?"

"Let's leave that up to your employer for now, shall we?"

Sydney's eye wanders to the upper right-hand corner of the Plan Options chart.

Blue Sky Insurance Company: Plan Options			
Plan Features	**HMO**	**PPO with low deductible**	**HDHP**
Deductible	0	$250	$3,000 individual **$6,000 family**
Coinsurance (Amount you pay after deductible)	0%	20%	0%
Out-of-pocket maximum (Total paid including deductible)	0	$3,000	$3,000 individual $6,000 family
Office visits (Copays not subject to deductible)	$10 copay	**$20 copay**	Pay full fee
Prescription brand-name drugs (Copays not subject to deductible)	$25 copay	$25 copay	Pay full fee
Annual exam (Office visit plus lab tests)	$100 copay	$100 copay	$100 copay

His expression shifts from sublime to shocked. "Wait a minute… this doesn't look good…a family deductible of $6,000! Why would any family want that plan?"

"Again, let's follow the money." Dave isolates a few lines near the bottom of the Blue Sky Insurance Premiums rate sheet.

Blue Sky Insurance Premiums (Age-rated and in dollars)			
	PPO	**HMO**	**HDHP**
Family			
under 30	805	885	290
30-39	**930**	1,040	380
40-49	1,025	1,115	490
50-54	1,215	1,250	515
50-59	1,475	1,385	650
60-64	1,860	1,680	770

"Look at family coverage for the 30-39 age group. With the HDHP you pay $380/month for protection against large medical bills. With the PPO you pay $930, an additional $550/month to receive the low deductible and various copays. You'd need a mighty sick little family to use all those bells and whistles."

"Let me see if I get it. If we used the HDHP instead of the PPO, and if we all stayed healthy, we'd save $550 per month in our health savings account, and over the course of a year that would be $6,600. Okay. I'm okay now. The deductible scared me off, but the savings definitely make it worthwhile. With three years of good health, we'd have more than $19,000 saved up against anything going wrong."

The Crusader smiles. "Something to keep in mind when the two of you start your own little family…which brings me to the most golden feature of the HSA, the lifetime of benefits. There are two ways to use an HSA. You can save money to spend it later, when you need to, or you can use it for current expenses."

"Consumers who are savers often strive to minimize medical use of the HSA in order to maximize savings for the future, particularly for healthcare expenses during retirement, building a large pool of tax-free money to pay expenses not covered by Medicare. If you maximize contributions and accumulate $200 per month in your HSA, you can use it as an investment vehicle, getting 6% return, and if it grows for 30 years until you reach age 65… Let's see, right under this stack I have a chart that shows what you'd have with only $100 per month invested tax-free." The Crusader shuffles his paperwork. "Here it is."

$100 Per Month with Different Rates ($)				
Years	**@ 0%**	**@ 2%**	**@ 4%**	**@ 6%**
5	6,000	6,304	6,629	6,977
10	12,000	13,271	14,724	16,387
15	18,000	20,971	24,609	29,081
20	24,000	29,479	36,677	46,204
25	30,000	38,882	51,412	69,299
30	36,000	49,272	69,404	**100,451**
35	42,000	60,754	91,373	142,471
40	48,000	73,443	118,196	199,140

"You would have over $100,000."

"This is for $100 per month, but you said I can contribute up to $200 per month?" asks Sydney, disbelieving. "I'd have *twice* that amount? Two hundred thousand, nine hundred and two?"

Lori leans forward. "Is that accurate?"

The Crusader grapples with his calculator. "Yes, $200,902 on the penny. Sydney, you've got a gift for calculations."

"He's a math wizard," brags Lorellei. "My good-lookin' Einstein."

"Okay, Einstein, let's say the interest rates get juicy. What will you get at 10%?"

Sydney looks at the chart on Dave's desk…

Years	@ 10%
5	7,744
10	20,484
15	41,447
20	75,930
25	132,683
30	**226,048**
35	379,663
40	632,408

…and smothers a smile. "Well, since I've been reading all your numbers upside-down from that sloppy pile on your desk, my guess is $226,048 times two, or $452,096. Unbelievable! Nearly half a million dollars in my HSA—is that possible?" Sydney reflects a moment. "Let me get this right. We can achieve this buildup in my HSA and still use my wife's HSA strictly for her healthcare?"

"Right. Even without Lori's help in funding those investments by age 65, you still come out smelling like a rose."

"Correct me if I'm wrong," interjects Lorellei, "but once we reach age 65, doesn't Medicare cover most of the expenses?"

"Yes and no. Medicare, shall we say, contains lots of little loopholes. Kind of like crossing a bog on a windy moonless night and hoping your feet don't hit quicksand. Experts—and here I'm quoting from Fidelity Investments—project that the average American couple will spend $191,000 of their own money on healthcare not covered by Medicare."

"So, what you're telling us," says Sydney, whose shoulders have begun to relax, "is that Lori will be taken care of medically, and I will be able to take care of us financially all the way through life if we start now, behave frugally, invest to the max and work on keeping ourselves as healthy as possible?"

"You got it."

Sydney stands to shake the Crusader's hand. "You told me I'd be feeling okay by the end of this meeting."

Dave smiles. "And I try to be a man of my word—you ready to meet the mysterious stranger I promised?" Dave leads them through the courtyard to the wide open doors of Scarlet O'Hara's, a robust, thriving retail store featuring women's clothing, shoes, bags, housewares and jewelry, all made my local artisans.

They hear the voice before they see the woman, a rich, warm combination of laughter and hard years. In her mid-fifties, she moves with a dancer's grace, and her eyes spark with untold stories. Her abundant shining hair is silver from tip to end, and everything about her glows with enthusiasm and energy. She is the embodiment of the phrase *good health*.

Dave makes the introductions. "Cassandra, meet Sydney and Lori. I'll leave you three to get to know each other."

Cassandra looks at Lori with compassion. "Life in that chair cannot be easy."

Lori feels tears behind her eyes and nods.

"Come with me." Cassandra leads them to a quiet back room and sends her assistant up front to cover the store. "I'm guessing the Crusader wants me to relate my story?" She smiles knowingly. "He brings someone about once a week. Please be comfortable.

"Twenty years ago I began to have major health complications. I'd been on the fast-track for a decade but suddenly I was so tired. My muscles were losing their strength, and I couldn't get out of bed. Life seemed pointless. I started going from one doctor to the next, saying, 'What is wrong with me?' No one could say. I had one test, then another, and finally so many I lost count. Then I lost my job, and, soon after, my insurance lapsed.

"I continued seeing doctor after doctor, but the tests couldn't pinpoint my condition. I couldn't make the payments on my condo. I lost that, too. I sold my BMW before it got repossessed and used the money to buy a metallic junker, a real 'rat on wheels.' This became my transportation and my home. I slept in the shabby back seat. I dug food out of dumpsters and begged on the streets until I didn't have the strength for more. Doctors avoided making appointments with me. I couldn't pay them. Eventually the parking lot at the beach became my front yard.

"One morning I awoke to a pack of bored kids trying to bust my car windows with baseball bats. They scattered when I sat up, but in that moment I knew I needed to take my life into my own hands or just take the long walk out into the ocean."

Cassandra leans fluidly against a table and wraps one leg easily beneath her. "That same day I used the last of my gas to drive my trusty junker up the mountain. I threw myself on the mercy of the Episcopalian monks up there, begging them to let me clean and cook in exchange for warm food and a safe place to sleep. They took me in."

Cassandra shakes her mane of hair fiercely, fighting back any tears of self-pity.

"Slowly, slowly, I got back my strength. I began reading from the library up there. I took strength from fresh air and my own brand of prayer. I started painting little watercolors on found scraps of paper—one of the monks lent me the paints—and after a while the little paintings started selling in the monastery bookstore.

"I got the courage to come down off the mountain, and I began my search for alternative care. The doctors hadn't helped, and I needed to understand what was wrong with me. In the end it was a twentieth century grab bag of women's complaints: herpes, chronic fatigue, depression, poor eating, stress.

"I found a naturopathic physician who let me work part-time as a receptionist in return for treatment. Slowly but surely I lost the person I once had been—hard drinking, hard selling and hard to live with. I lost all my money, too, but I regained my soul. Little by little I saw my health returning and I remained steadfast on the path of alternative life.

"And now here I am, with you. Two lovely young people. Confusion all over your faces. Fear. You have a right to feel it. I guess the lesson I'm trying to relate is this: I had to find the path to my own health. The doctors couldn't show me. Without charity and self-help, I would not have made it.

"My traditional PPO insurance—while I still had it—would never have paid for my crazy system of good health. But an HSA will. That health savings account is your ticket to independent life, Lori. I'm not saying my path will free you of your fate, but it freed me of mine. With an HSA, at least you have the freedom to seek alternative means. You are no longer stuck with only one road to health."

Cassandra waits as a myriad of emotions floods Lorellei's face. She turns demurely away as Sydney deals with his tears.

"I can help with resources, if you ever need me."

"Thank you," whispers Lorellei. Sydney can only nod in gratitude. The couple leaves with Cassandra watching and smiling, knowing they will prevail.

The HSA Crusader shouts from his office. "Wait! About your article! After you left I realized I hadn't finished. The HDHP and HSA can successfully insure the bulk of Americans, but our government is going to have to step in with a safety net—"

"—to catch those who fall through the cracks. Exactly," adds Lorellei. "That was my last question: how?"

"Lori, I don't know how. In our current system, the poor are taken care of, but it is hugely inefficient, and of a quality that most of us would not accept. We need someone possessed of a far vision. Whoever that person turns out to be has got my vote."

"Me, too," admits Lorellei. Sydney stands close behind her, his hands on her wheelchair. "Yes," he adds. "Hear, hear."

* * * * * * *

It is the end of a long day. The office of the presidential hopeful has emptied of assistants, attachés, tourists, hangers-on and lobbyists. A last minute check of e-mails before logging out to go home stops the legislator in mid-act. On the screen is a message from an insurance agent calling himself the HSA Crusader. In a few brief words he explains he is a proponent of the consumer-directed health plans "…but I've been in an agony over this last missing piece of the puzzle."

HDHP + HSA + [HELP?] = SOLUTION

The formula floats on the screen. The legislator seems frozen, staring as one word seems to vibrate and lift free of the others.

HELP

Suddenly, hands lift free of the keyboard as the legislator stands. *This is the missing link.* Hands shaking with excitement, the presidential hopeful throws on a jacket, hurries out of the office and hails a cab. Carrying its sole passenger, the taxi sprints up Connecticut Avenue.

At the home of Matt's parents, Bev and Laurence, there is a lull in the conversation, accentuated by a sudden banging on the stately door. Matt excuses himself from a small gathering of intimate friends and moves to the entryway. He opens the door to find his mentor standing breathless on the porch.

"Matt, I've got it, the key word is *help*. Help for the needy. Single payer to the needy! I was—my, you're certainly looking formal—is that a new suit? I was sitting, staring, well, staring at an e-mail, actually, and suddenly there it was right in front of me…so simple, I can't believe we didn't see it. I—oh, hi, Bev. Hi Laurence. Great to see you—goodness, you're all looking so glamorous, I—oh dear, you're having an event. I'm so sorry…I've interrupted. Here, Matt, we'll talk tomorrow."

"Nonsense, come in!"

"I couldn't."

"I insist."

"Oh, well, fine. I'm not really dressed properly. It's just that I had such great news for you."

"And Matt has great news for you," says Bev, stepping forward to greet her childhood friend warmly.

Invited into the cozy living room, the legislator is introduced to an elegant young woman with piercing eyes. Matt steps forward enthusiastically, "Actually, your timing is impeccable. I've just gotten myself engaged—successfully. Meet my fiancée, Kristina, and her Uncle Carl from the Treasury."

"Kristina, my pleasure and best wishes. Carl. I've read your work."

"We have an hour to kill before our dinner reservation," interjects Laurence, "if you need to speak with Matt."

"No, I couldn't intrude. Matt, stop by to see me, early tomorrow."

"Nonsense," booms Matt's father.

"Come in for a while," says Kristina. "Frankly, we were all starting to get a little edgy sitting around here smiling at each other."

"And," adds Carl, "I'm dying to know what has you hopping around so enthusiastically—if you're free to divulge."

"Well—really? I'd love to share it," admits the legislator, accepting a glass of champagne, "I can't take full credit. Matt and I and a thousand others have been circling this problem for years, but I think I've found the ballast to right our ship in the water."

"Your ship?" echoes Laurence.

"The USS Healthcare," explains Kristina. "Matt has kept me informed along the way. You've discovered the missing piece of the healthcare puzzle, haven't you?"

"Why, yes. I hope so. I've spent months of sleepless nights trying to choose between government-sponsored healthcare and the free market alternative. Then I get this e-mail, and suddenly there it is, so clear I wonder that I never saw it."

"And that would be?" The party waits for the answer to Kristina's question.

"Our job is not to choose *between* the alternatives, but to fuse the opposing forces and thereby create an entirely new entity—consumer-directed healthcare fused with the single-payer idea."

"The USS Healthcare," whispers Matt, the power of the idea dawning. "Yes! It isn't Canadian, it isn't European, and it definitely isn't a sinking ship. It's American-style healthcare we can all trust."

"Well put," compliments his mentor. "We need a system to care for everyone. But to bankrupt America is not to care for her. So…we need the free market to float the bulk of the healthcare solution. And we need government to fill in the gaps."

"Wait," says Matt. "I get it. Single payer *to* the needy. Brilliant."

"Yes," says his mentor, eyes lighting. "Instead of government directly paying healthcare providers who dole out and ration services as in Canada, we switch government's role. Instead of paying medical bills *for* the needy, the government gives money directly *to* the needy to purchase a high-deductible health plan. In the same way, the government gives money to fund a Health Savings Account for each person who cannot afford it."

"Won't they abuse the system?" asks Laurence.

"What?" challenges Bev, "You're gonna penalize Uncle Sam just because a few nieces and nephews don't know how to behave?"

"Of course there will be abuse," says Carl matter-of-factly, "but the voucher system will ameliorate most of it. Disadvantaged Americans deserve their dignity. Most of us want to choose our own healthcare and have sufficient means to pay for it."

"It chops the bureaucracy in half, at least," adds Kristina.

"Here's the thing," says the presidential hopeful. "We Americans are a fair-minded and independent group. If we can afford something, we are happy to pay for it. Also, we want a system that helps those who can't afford health insurance."

"And this is it," says Matt with feeling. "You're coupling consumer-directed healthcare with single-payer healthcare—the best of the political right and the best of the political left. Brilliant."

Following a brief rush of questions, the future candidate realizes a powerful need to be alone. At the door, Matt shakes the hand of his mentor, who meets his eyes. "Couldn't have done it without you, Matt."

"Hey, you're not done with me. Master and disciple. Body and shadow."

"'Body and shadow?' Matt, we need to debrief you of your California experience."

Matt grins. "Permission requested to make phone calls to five hundred of your staunchest supporters?"

"Permission granted—and invite the people who think they hate me, too. Finally, I have that all-important announcement to make."

"Your wish is my command, Prez."

The presidential hopeful steps lightly down a stair and turns, raising two fingers in a well-known gesture. "Hey, Matt…peace."

"Huh? Oh, yeah. Peace and, uh, victory, too—dude."

CHAPTER SIX

A Candidate for All Seasons

From the back of a large hall, Matt listens to the echo of his mentor's voice as it rings over the audience. "…healthcare, healthcare, healthcare. Now you know my platform. I'm going to own it, I'm going to run with it to the very end and anyone who wants to help, sign up here because we are going to need you."

Matt raises his binoculars for a closer look and sees the familiar face, imbued with strength and humor. He's familiar with the speech, yet doesn't want to miss a single word.

"That said, I admit we do not have much agreement on what help is needed, though even extremists agree we must repair our increasingly dysfunctional healthcare system. Something is terribly wrong at the heart of things when the citizens of a great country do not universally enjoy abundant health and well-being. Here's what I see:

- Health insurance premiums consistently spiral upward out of control.
- Healthcare costs rise at two to three times normal inflation, compared to all other products and services in our country.
- One in six American citizens does not have health insurance coverage, and many cite the high cost of insurance as the reason.
- Experts predict that the cost of healthcare for the baby boomers will bankrupt America, and even with all of this, we are now an open door for diabetes, cancer, heart disease and many other serious, life-threatening diseases.

"These failures affect every single one of us, and I do not exaggerate when I say healthcare is the number one domestic issue in the upcoming presidential election. So what can we do? This is America, a nation known for both diversity and unity. Remember, we have named ourselves the *United* States of America. Best of the blue, best of the red—and all the shades in between.

"I think both sides might vote for dignity, choice and well-being. I think both agree we want affordable access to quality healthcare for every member of our families. Perhaps we need to think of our nation as a family, with everyone pulling their own weight as far as possible.

"As I have already made clear, I am against the single-payer plans of Canada and Europe. We hear too many horror stories of health rationing. A pure welfare state gives us desperate citizens who stand in line for the dole. What could be more dehumanizing? Alternatively, unbridled free enterprise gives us the Love Canal scandal, Arctic plunder, the end of rain forests and ultimately the dreaded specter of global warming.

"Neither works for the United States. We need our own solution, not an echo of Canada or Europe but a nonpartisan offering. Toward that end, I would like to propose American-style healthcare, and it works like this.

"For those who stand to the right of me, I agree we need to reintroduce competition to the healthcare world. Our current system is clearly not free market. For all intents and purposes, we have a managed-care system where negotiated fees for healthcare providers are controlled by insurance companies. While an individual may know her copay, she rarely knows the real costs of healthcare services. This is like going into a store to purchase a pair of shoes and being told you have to buy them before being informed of the price.

"In our current system, Americans pay about sixteen cents for every dollar of healthcare they buy, which makes it much closer to a government-run program than a market-based program, and we see how hugely ineffective this has been.

"Government's role should be to create an environment that will foster free market competition—it works well for the rest of the economy, and can work well for healthcare. To make our Red states happy, I propose three policies conducive to healthcare reform.

"First, make all health insurance tax deductible. Currently, businesses and self-employed individuals receive a tax deduction for insurance premiums. Unfairly, non-self-employed individuals, who must purchase their own insurance, do not. We need to devise a uniform policy.

"The second policy I recommend is to use insurance for large unexpected bills. Encourage health insurance companies to provide affordable insurance protection from large, unexpected bills, just like home or auto insurance. Statistics show that the majority of Americans can afford either a $1,000, $2,000 or $3,000 deductible plan. To help, make high-deductible health plan premiums 100% tax deductible.

"And the third policy? My hope is that Americans plan and save for a lifetime of better health. Armed with HSAs, consumers will have the ammunition to shop for the best values in healthcare based upon quality, service and price. Research tells us that up to three-fourths of all Americans spend $500 per year or less, allowing for tremendous savings potential. By switching from traditional to high-deductible plans, these Americans can save 20 to 60% on premiums. To strongly encourage investment of those savings we must continue the generous tax benefits of the HSA—tax-deductible contributions, tax-free growth and tax-free withdrawals for healthcare.

"These tax benefits, plus the ability to use the HSA to save for healthcare expenses over a lifetime, provide good incentives to those people who can afford insurance but currently opt out for one reason or another.

"With the consumer paying routine bills, our doctors, laboratories, hospitals and pharmaceutical companies are liberated to compete for consumer dollars, controlling healthcare costs at their proper level just as with every other product or service in America. Entrepreneurs will introduce more innovative products and services to increase market share.

"Now, for those who stand to the left of me, I am not abandoning those who advocate a larger role for government, who appreciate the charms of the single-payer plan, but I do have some new ideas.

"Granted, it is intuitively pleasing to have the government collect taxes and make this tax money available in the form of universal 'free' healthcare. In fact, it seems Utopian. But, trust me, there is rain in Camelot. It is a proven fact that, if you collect taxes and give 'free' care, people will access the system more frequently. In order to hold down costs, a government must ration the more expensive care. This rationing is greater as we get older, with a 65-year-old in need of a transplant having a lower priority than a 30-year-old. Do we really want this?

There is a large rumbling as the crowd considers this aloud. The candidate waits for the room to quiet before resuming.

"We Americans are a fair-minded and independent group. On the whole, if we can afford healthcare, we are happy to pay for it. Most of us are also concerned to help the less fortunate and the truly needy. Even selfishly, we realize that but for the grace of God we might be wheelchair-bound or a single mother working three jobs.

"Therefore, let America do what she does best—carry the eternal torch and come to the aid of those in need. Instead of a single payer plan for all Americans, I propose three policies which, tied together, form one system which I call Single Payer TO The Needy.

"We need to empower the working poor and the truly needy to participate in the new American healthcare alliance. Currently in the free Medicaid system, you have a long wait to see a very limited number of doctors who often have only a small amount of time to spend with you. Over the years, reimbursement to healthcare providers has systematically diminished. Most healthcare providers will not see Medicaid patients—something the rest of America would not tolerate. Let's not ask the poor to jump through these hoops.

"The weakest link of the healthcare chain are those who currently participate in programs such as Medicaid and State Children's Health Insurance Programs. This 12% of our population needs our continuing support but, for goodness sake, need to receive it with dignity. To paraphrase our country's renowned economist, John Kenneth Galbraith, 'Government exists to humanize capitalism.'

"To make the Blue states happy, I propose the following three programs:

- **All America Insured.** For disadvantaged individuals and families, as an option to placing federal and state money into the Medicaid program, I propose vouchers to purchase fully-paid high-deductible health plans and fully funded health savings accounts. In pilot studies, this approach appears much more cost-effective and easy to administer than traditional Medicaid programs. Participants have money to choose doctors and are no longer limited to providers who accept Medicaid. Hospitals are paid outright for services. This ends the practice whereby, having received insufficient reimbursement from the government, these hospitals turn around and overcharge insured patients to make up for what Medicaid did not pay.
- **Working to Make America Great.** This is not a cliché but a program for the working poor who have jobs but are unable to afford the total cost of health insurance premiums. It will create refundable tax credits for that portion of a high-deductible health plan and Health Savings Account which that individual or family is unable to pay. This guarantees protection from large, unexpected healthcare expenses and also guarantees money to pay for routine healthcare.
- **Insurance for a Lifetime.** As an option to the current Medicare plan, let's enable seniors to direct Medicare dollars to purchase high-deductible health plans and to fund Health Savings Accounts. Currently the government is pilot testing this idea, giving seniors total freedom in their choice of physician or hospital.

As the candidate takes a moment to shift gears, the crowd quiets. Kristina arrives late, and Matt whispers, "Good. You're just in time for the best part."

The candidate takes a deep breath before saying, "Thank you all for hanging in here with me. I'd like to take you somewhere a little bit off the beaten path, now. Somewhere a little bit visionary, if I may. The foregoing suggestions give us a good place to start in combining the wishes of Blue states and Red states, the wishes of all Americans, and do much to create an environment of change, but ultimately they are not what will save us.

"At the bottom of this whole big healthcare argument is the simple, universal desire to be well, to enjoy abundant health and happy lives, regardless of the party you vote for. If we keep leaning on doctors to deliver us our health on a gurney, we will continue to spiral down. People of America, what is our true goal? Is it the widespread care of illness, or is it the pursuit of vibrant, electrifying health?

"In the traditional healthcare model, you must have a medical condition before insurance will pay. I say this is upside-down. I say we should be rewarded for good health, be enabled to fund our own healthcare choices, to have the assurance of catastrophic coverage and to engender self-reliance.

"Picture what could happen if every American were to strive for optimum health? What if 50% of all adults and children were to improve their health 50% within five years? We would be rewarded with healthier, happier, calmer, brighter and more generous children, teenagers, college students and adults.

"Imagine the change this might bring about in our society. After all, who we are as individuals does determine the fate of our nation. The attitude at the core of our being ripples outward, like it or not, from self to family to community to nation to world.

"Trust me, the solution to our healthcare crisis is also the solution to our impending economic crisis. Retiring baby-boomers for the next four generations will put a huge load on our existing systems. We need to retrench and redesign—now. At this very moment in history, we need to rethink the meaning of health. And for this we need to be united as a nation. Right now our government is hard at work renovating Medicare, helping that agency to better serve our nation. I say we can do this at every level, this renovation of the spirit of things.

"What if we were to eat for our health, exercise for our health, worship, work, raise our families and reach to the very edge of entrepreneurial genius with an attitude of health? Why, we could revitalize the world.

"May I be so bold as to suggest that as a nation we adopt a universal attitude of wellness? And once we have our health at an enviable level, by generously funding our HSAs, we can provide a future of stability and resource, especially in our declining years."

The candidate pauses to allow the idea to grasp the minds of the audience members before continuing. "And let's not stop there. In the exploding arena of technology, let's inspire and reward those who give us clean, 'green' industries. Our dependence on foreign oil is as antiquated as our current healthcare system.

"As far as enterprise, our goal should be to build, advance and incorporate, but not to plunder. Look over your shoulder to your children and grandchildren. Let's encourage innovative young developers who seek to improve the intrinsic quality of daily life.

"In the environment, we should look seriously at this issue of sustainability and see how we might make it profitable. Supporting and participating in local agriculture may be one of the best forms of homeland security. It diminishes our reliance on foreign oil, restores local economies, rebuilds healthy soils, recycles nutrients and water, improves personal health and increases the pleasure of the dinner table.

"It is antiquated thinking that says our economic prosperity must exclude physical and mental well-being. We need to strike out upon this fresh course, but ultimately it is the traditional dream of America toward independence and self-sufficiency, true prosperity and a lasting peace.

"John F. Kennedy envisioned a nation of the most healthy, the best educated, the most benevolent and worthy of respect. His immortal words, spoken half a century ago, still resound with the fresh vigor of a nation looking boldly toward the future. 'Ask not what your country can do for you...ask what you can do for your country.' Let us move toward that sterling goal, all of us. Let us win back the United States with health, dignity, economy and benevolence."

Matt and Kristina applaud with the rest of the crowd in the hall.

"I would like to close with the following words, passed down through time from the philosopher, Goethe. He has this to tell us...

> The moment one definitely commits oneself, then Providence moves too. All sorts of things occur to help one that would never otherwise have occurred. A whole stream of events issues from the decision, raising in one's favor all manner of unforeseen incidents and meetings and material assistance, which no man could have dreamed would have come his way..."

At this, Matt stands and joins his voice with that of the person he hopes one day will be President.

> "Whatever you can do, or dream you can do, begin it. Boldness has genius, power, and magic in it. Begin it now."

In closing, to the accompaniment of heartfelt applause, the candidate delivers final words. "Thank you, all of you, for your continuing support. Now, if you will all roll back your sleeves, we have a nation to awaken! Let us give each other good health!"

"Here, here," Matt says to Kristina, as the lights begin to fade.

Effective 1-1-07, Six New Health Savings Accounts Benefits Were Passed Into Law by Congress

Historically, consumers have paid rent money for health insurance premiums, and had nothing to show for it at the end of the year. Health Savings Accounts were passed into law late in 2003, so now you may own some of that rent money by putting it into a special savings account for health care. HSAs enable you to pay for current health expenses and save for future qualified medical and retiree health expenses on a tax-free basis. HSAs have triple tax benefits --- tax-deductible contributions, tax-free growth of interest, and tax-free withdrawals for healthcare. This is the only way to save money truly tax-free.

In December, 2006, H.R. 6111, The Tax Relief and Health Care Act of 2006 was signed into law. The six changes are significant and afford consumers the opportunity to save 20 to 60% on health insurance premiums and collectively save billions of dollars each year in Health Savings Accounts.

- Under the new law, companies and/or individuals can now contribute the full amount ($2,850 per individual or $5,650 per family in 2007) to their HSA, even if the deductible is a lesser amount.

- It allows one-time transfers from IRAs. Another provision allows one-time rollovers of Flexible Spending Accounts (FSAs) and Health Reimbursement Accounts (HRAs) into the HSAs.

- Companies can now contribute a higher amount (up to $2,850 for individuals and $5,650 for families for 2007) to HSAs of lower paid workers and lesser amounts to higher paid workers.

- Consumers can start HSAs at anytime during the year and still be able to put the maximum amount allowed into the HSAs, instead of prorating the amount as they had to do in the past.

- The Treasury Department must announce Cost of Living Increases (COLAs) in June, instead of November as previously done. This will give everyone more time to design HSA strategies for the upcoming year.

See full details of the new law at:

http://thomas.loc.gov/cgi-bin/query/F?c109:6:./temp/~c109D2t2Et:e92249:

Debra and Robert Hopper, Bio

Debra is a fiction writer. Bob owns a health insurance business and is the author of the textbook, The HSA Strategy: the Future of Healthcare in America.

Both have a passion for politics and social justice, and dinner conversations can grow quite lively with Debra leaning a little to the left and Bob, a little to the right.

Along with too many cats and dogs, they make their home in sunny southern California.